the shame of war

sexual violence against women and girls in conflict

IRIN

Office for the Coordination of Humanitarian Affairs
Integrated Regional Information Networks

A United Nations OCHA/IRIN publication

Contributing writers:	Jeanne Ward	Chapter 1
	Christopher Horwood	Chapter 2 & 4
	Claire McEvoy	Chapter 3 & 5
	Pamela Shipman & Lauren Rumble	Chapter 6

Contributing photographers: Guillaume Bonn, Georgina Cranston, Jan Dago, Manoocher Deghati, Mariella Furrer, Thomas Grabka, Evelyn Hochstein, Eddie Isango, Jerry Lampen, Anthony Lloyd, Sylvia Spring, Brent Stirton, Jennifer Szymaszek, Sven Torfinn, Francesco Zizola, Tiggy Ridley.

Project manager and book design: Christopher Horwood

Sub-editor Lisa Ernst
Layout: Eugene Papa, Publishing Services Section
United Nations Office at Nairobi
Printing: Progress Press Co. Ltd. Malta. February 2007

Cover photo and caption: Two victims of rape in Darfur comfort each other. Amnesty International's 2004 report on Sudan – Darfur, Rape as a Weapon of War – revealed that rape was widespread and often systematic. According to its findings, "In many cases the women have been raped in public, in front of their husbands, relatives or the wider community. Those who have resisted rapes were reportedly beaten, stabbed or killed. Girls as young as eight years old have been abducted and held in sexual slavery, some for many months." Three years later, reports from Darfur maintain the rapes have not stopped, despite the presence of thousands of international aid workers, thousands of African Union monitors and countless protests to the Sudanese government.
Image: Evelyn Hockstein

IRIN

Provides humanitarian news and analysis, through on-line articles, special reports, printed publications, film documentaries and radio. IRIN is part of the United Nations Office for the Coordination of Humanitarian Affairs (OCHA). For more information visit: www.irinnews.org

For specific information concerning this publication contact: shameofwar@irinnews.org

SOLDIERS

They come from a land where soldiers control each spot and not
One woman's body is free

Woman once sacred flower blossom to dawn
Slowly devoured until life inside of her is gone
Exterior wasted
Been tasted by too many men
Slapped pinned down again and again and
There is no exit from this trap
Pools of blood in the center of her lap
Dripping into cracked spaces
Covering once beautiful faces
Embraces
Have no place here
The land where sex breeds fear and
Babies are born out of torn wombs
Woman they pray cry out to the moon
For there can be no God
Who watches their pain and remains
Still
Like they are
Still
Being beaten with whips
Still
Being torn apart each night by a different poet stick
And they
Still
Watch their mothers dip their hands below Earth tears

This is the land where soldiers control each spot and not
One woman's body is free

by Imani Woomera

Acknowledgements

This publication is IRIN's second book on aspects of gender-based violence and part of OCHA / IRIN's longer term commitment to this issue by offering products to increase awareness of and information about different forms of violence against women and girls.

Special thanks go to the photographer Brent Stirton, who contributed many of his outstanding images used in this publication free of charge. We thank all the photographers who collected images and testimonies while on assignment. Our greatest appreciation, however, goes to the women and girls featured in this book who consented to share their personal stories with us. These women have suffered, and will continue to suffer, different forms of violence and deserve far more support and protection.

The project was generously supported by two donors : the Swiss Agency for Development And Cooperation and Global Fund for Women financed through the Forum for Early Warning and Early Response (FEWER).

contents

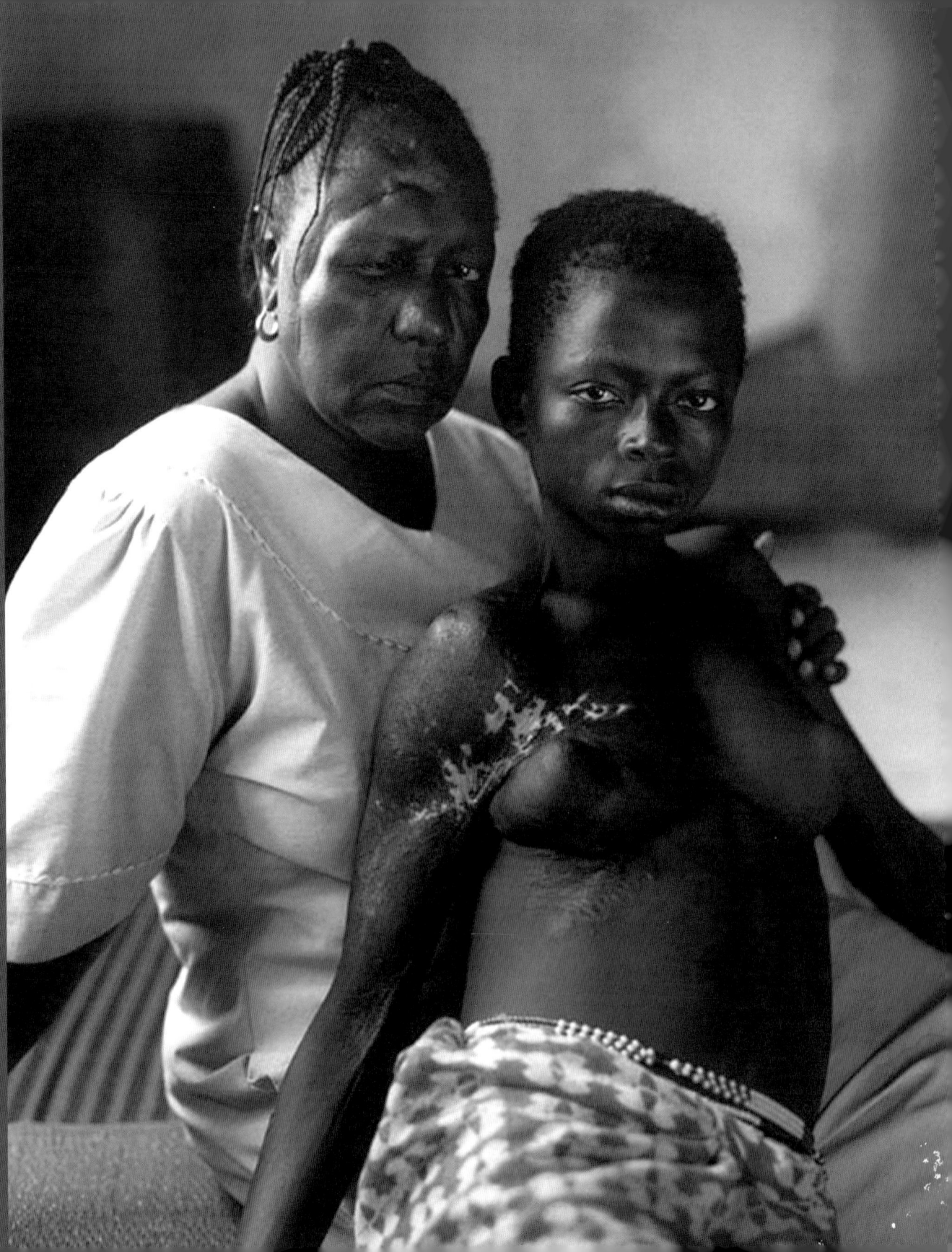

Two victims of sexual abuse and torture. The older woman, a nurse by profession, was abducted by rebels in Sierra Leone to live as a "bush wife". The scar on her forehead is from a bullet wound she sustained when the soldiers, after gang-raping her, tortured her by seeing how close they could come to killing her with an AK-47. The younger woman a former "bush wife" in Sierra Leone, who was abducted from her family at age 10 by rebels from the Revolutionary United Front. After a killing spree that decimated most of her village, the rebels took her away with them to work as a cook, porter and sex slave. When she tried to escape, the rebels poured acid over her arm and breast as a warning to other abductees. After two years in captivity, she was able to escape. She recently joined a small self-help group of female torture victims.

Image: Brent Stirton

the shame of war

sexual violence against women and girls in conflict

In this age of unprecedented communication and international mobility, the ugly truths of wars can no longer remain hidden and obscure. Journalistic reporting, documentaries, investigations, research and commissions of inquiry are exposing the violence of yesterday and demanding accountability and redress. People are finding the voice to speak out and, increasingly, the world is listening. In particular, women are making themselves and their sufferings heard. Throughout the centuries of human conflict, armies have sexually abused and enslaved women and girls with complete impunity, in what some may have seen as the natural process of war; but the tide is turning. The international community, now more united in its aspirational commitment to universal human rights, no longer finds these abuses to be acceptable or inevitable. Rape and sexual exploitation of women in times of conflict should never be tolerated, let alone excused.

The brutality and viciousness of the sexual attacks that are reported from the current conflicts in Democratic Republic of Congo, Myanmar, Iraq and Sudan, and the testimonies from past conflicts in Timor-Leste, Liberia, the Balkans and Sierra Leone are heartbreaking. Girls and women, old and young, are preyed upon by soldiers, militia, police and armed thugs wherever conflict rages and the parties to the conflict fail to protect civilian populations.

We need to wage a different war, one against violence against women and girls and against the culture of impunity that protects the perpetuators and their accomplices. To some extent, this battle is already underway, but it is in its very early days. People around the world, shocked at the revelations from conflict zones, are becoming motivated and engaged to look for ways to end impunity and create effective legal mechanisms that protect women and deny perpetrators sanctuary from prosecution and punishment.

Within my capacity as the UN Special Rapporteur on violence against women, its causes and consequences, I have seen that violence against women in times of armed conflict is merely the tip of the iceberg. The problem is so deep-rooted and widespread in all societies – in times of war and in peace – that one is sometimes left with a sense of despair and helplessness as to where to begin. But the trajectories of women's struggles to resist violence and oppression worldwide demonstrate that violence against women can be and must be stopped. We must act and we must act with a sense of urgency to address the entire continuum of violence against women and the gender hierarchies within which the problem is embedded.

The Shame of War: Sexual Violence Against Women and Girls in Conflict bears witness through graphic photographs and powerful testimonies to the scale of sexual violence faced by girls and women in conflicts all over the world. It pulls no punches in confronting the reader with stories and statistics that expose the extent of these violations that define countless women's and girls' everyday existence. It also charts the progress made in international law in recent years in protecting women's rights and convicting perpetrators of rape and sexual violence.

This book serves to raise awareness and provoke action. I would like to end by echoing the powerful words from the preface to Broken Bodies, Broken Dreams, an earlier book by IRIN on gender-based violence: History will judge us harshly if, once aware of the nature and scope of this violence, once outraged by its injustice, we do not choose to act against it.

Yakın Ertürk, Prof of Sociology and
UN Special Rapporteur on Violence against Women, its causes and consequences

introduction

" We need to voice the violence, to hear the stories of all those affected by violence … Spreading the word, breaking down the taboos and exposing the violence that takes place among us is the first step towards effective action to reduce violence in our own societies."

Gro Harlem Brundtland, former prime minister of Norway and former director general of the World Health Organization

This book was born out of shock. It was also born out of the research and extraordinary testimonies collected for a previous publication on gender-based violence produced at the end of 2005. The photo/reference book Broken Bodies - Broken Dreams: Violence against women exposed is a work of analysis and reportage combined with personal testimonies, case studies and extensive use of photography, covering all aspects of gender-based violence. During the development of that publication, it became clear that the issue of sexual violence in times of conflict and post-conflict was in need of urgent attention. Readers of both publications will find some areas of deliberate duplication and overlap.

Too long left unexposed and considered a natural or unavoidable aspect of war, the practice of mass rape and brutal sexual torture of women and girls in conflict has to be challenged.

The culture of conflict and the culture of impunity that allow rapes and sexual torture to continue need to be exposed, and as a world community we need to be outraged and motivated to respond. We need to understand the nature of the problem and the origins of our collective discrimination and persecution of women during war, and understand how change can take place.

The aspirations, expectations and behaviour of people and societies concerning human rights has changed dramatically in recent decades. It is a positive process that has only just begun and has many more battles to be won. There is reason to believe that, with sufficient political will and increased exposure of the unacceptable nature of sexual violence against civilians in conflict, a massive reduction in the number of these crimes can be achieved in the coming years. In the meantime, there is much that can be done to assist the millions of women and girls who live

the shame of war

sexual violence against women and girls in conflict

with the legacy of their violations, their physical and mental damage, the economic destitution and frequent social dislocation.

This book's primary focus is on sexual crimes in war, its impact on women's lives, and efforts to turn the tide against the practise of using women's bodies as battlegrounds. Chapter one outlines the scope and nature of sexual violence in war, particularly against vulnerable non-combatants such as refugees and internally displaced persons. It includes harrowing personal testimonies and discussion of the medical impact of rape, the culture of impunity and the lack of institutional support. This chapter is taken directly from the book Broken Bodies - Broken Dreams (Chapter 13), where it is titled, Sexual Violence in Times of War.

Chapter two outlines different ideas about what motivates rapists in war; the special characteristics of combatants and the dangers for women and girls. It looks at different ideologies surrounding rape, especially at how applying the theory that rape is used as part of political and military strategies has assisted in convictions and prosecutions.

The third chapter discusses the urgent need to challenge and counter the culture of impunity of rape in war. It looks at recent developments in international law as well as important new judicial precedents. It outlines the key legal instruments in international humanitarian law, including human rights law.

Sexual exploitation and abuse by United Nations peacekeepers and international aid workers has attracted considerable media coverage and concern. In so far as these acts take place in conflict or post-conflict contexts, it has been included in this publication. Chapter four features two articles on sexual exploitation or abuse by peacekeepers and international UN and humanitarian agency staff and considers how the sector is responding.

The last two chapters focus on the question of post-conflict justice and the deficiencies in the international community's response to the issue. Seeking Post-Conflict Justice, chapter five, looks at the different mechanisms being used to provide some level of justice for victims of sexual attack. It focuses on the non-judicial mechanisms of truth commissions. Chapter six, to end, examines the enormous challenge facing the world with respect to assisting those who survive rape and sexual violence during war. It discusses post-traumatic medical assistance needs, the social responses to rape, and the need for economic support for women who survive rape, as well as addressing their psychosocial needs. This chapter discusses some of the efforts being made in this direction, some of the international infrastructure/commitment to respond and, lastly, the failure to address the issues properly. In outlining the areas of neglect, it also challenges readers to do more.

"Safety and security don't just happen: they are the result of collective consensus and public investment. We owe our children – the most vulnerable citizens in any society – a life free from violence and fear. In order to ensure this, we must become tireless in our efforts not only to attain peace, justice and prosperity for countries but also for communities and members of the same family. We must address the roots of violence. Only then will we transform the past century's legacy from a crushing burden into a cautionary lesson."

Nelson Mandela, World Report on Violence and Health 2002

Bemguema in Sierra Leone, 2002. A young girl, followed by women from her village, passes a group of soldiers from the national army on break from training. The war in Sierra Leone gained notoriety for the level of atrocities committed against civilians by gangs of young men and boys, who often were high on drugs and alcohol. The gangs were linked to different militia or rebel factions, and they raped, mutilated and killed thousands of civilians.

Image: Jan Dago

Chapter 1

sexual violence against women and girls in conflict

International Rescue Committee stated in August 2006, "More than 200 women have been sexually assaulted in the last five weeks alone around Darfur's largest displaced camp, Kalma [...] This is a massive spike in figures. We are used to hearing of 2 to 4 incidents of sexual assault per month in Kalma camp."

During and following a rebel offensive launched in 1998 on the capital city of Brazzaville in the Republic of Congo, approximately 2,000 women sought medical treatment for sexual violence; 10 percent of them reported rape-related pregnancies.[1] UN officials estimate the real number of women who were raped in Brazzaville during this single wave of violence to be closer to 5,000.[2]

The changing face of war

A growing body of data from the wars of the last decade is finally bringing to light "one of history's great silences": the sexual violation and torture of civilian women and girls during periods of armed conflict.[3] Until recently, the evidence – along with the issue – had been generally ignored by historians, politicians and the world at large, yet it is hardly new. The licence of victors to "rape and pillage" the vanquished dates back to ancient Greek, Roman and Hebrew wars.[4] In examples from the last century alone, Jewish women were raped by Cossacks during the 1919 pogroms in Russia; the Japanese military trafficked thousands of "comfort women" from countries across Asia and sexually enslaved them during World War II; more than 100,000 women were raped in the Berlin area directly following World War II; and hundreds of thousands of Bengali women were raped by Pakistani soldiers during the 1971 Bangladeshi war of secession.[5]

Despite the history of sexual violence committed against women by men in times of war, what is especially disturbing about the statistics from the past 10 years is how rife the phenomenon appears to have become. It might be argued that the current data simply reflect greater international attention to the issue – provoked in part by the media coverage of the sexual atrocities committed during the conflicts in the former Yugoslavia and Rwanda, and even more importantly by the decades of intensive awareness-raising by women's activists around the world – rather than a significant rise in absolute numbers of victims. A more likely explanation, however, is that the nature of warfare is changing in ways that increasingly endanger women and girls.

Since the latter half of the last century, combat primarily limited to military engagements between national armies has been largely supplanted by civil wars and regional conflicts that pit communities along racial, religious and/or ethnic lines. The result is that civilian populations are victimised on a massive scale. Between 1989 and 1997, an estimated 103 armed conflicts were launched in 69 countries across the world.[6] Civilian casualties during these more recent conflicts are estimated to be as high as 75 percent, a stunning contrast to the 5 percent estimate from the start of the last century.[7] Although overall more men than women continue to die as a result of conflict, women and girls suffer myriad debilitating consequences of war.[8] So much so, according to a 2002 report of the Secretary-General of the United Nations, that "women and children are disproportionately targets" and "constitute the majority of all victims" of contemporary armed conflicts.[9]

What the current data conceal

However disturbing the current statistics are, they probably conceal more than they reveal in terms of the true extent of sexual violence against women and girls during armed conflict. For a number of reasons, data on rape in war is exceedingly difficult to capture – as seen in the sometimes dramatic variance in estimates from any given country, such as those from Bosnia that range from 14,000 to 50,000, and from Rwanda that range from 15,700 to a half-million.[10] Sometimes the discrepancies reflect political interests, where a government or armed group may seek to downplay the extent of crimes committed by its members, while others are working to highlight those crimes. Yet even when research is undertaken by nonaligned human rights or other groups, obtaining an accurate representation of the scope of sexual violence presents tremendous challenges.

Research on sexual violence against women during war is in its relative infancy. Investigators have only just begun to develop and test methodologies for collecting representative data. In addition, substantial underreporting of rape is commonplace even in times of peace; in times of war and its aftermath, when constraining factors such as stigma and shame are compounded by political instability and threats to personal safety, rates of reporting are likely to be even lower. Exposing violence in the context of active conflict can represent a security risk for all involved – as evidenced by the May 2005 arrest of the Médecins Sans Frontières (MSF) head of mission in Khartoum, Sudan, who was charged by the Sudanese government with crimes against the state after publishing a report on women seeking rape-related medical treatment at MSF facilities throughout Darfur.[11]

In many more instances, there is simply no institutional authority or organisation to whom a woman can recount her experience. Even where services do exist, pervasive impunity for perpetrators of war-related sexual violence means that many survivors may accurately reason that no

However disturbing the current statistics are, they probably conceal more than they reveal in terms of the true extent of sexual violence against women and girls during armed conflict.

justice – and thus no purpose would be served by reporting the crime. Notably, in a 2001 study from Timor-Leste, only 7 percent of women who had experienced physical or sexual violence during the crisis of 1999 ever reported their victimisation to a local authority.[12] In a survey from Rwanda, only 6 percent of respondents who had been raped during the genocide ever sought medical treatment.[13]

The current statistics – detached as they are from the nature of the crimes – do not reveal the depths of violence to which women and girls have been exposed, or the terror they are forced to endure when their bodies become the ways and means of war. It is only the personal accounts that do this – accounts that most of the world will likely never hear.

Three personal stories

Since the 1996 outbreak of hostilities among multiple armed factions in eastern Democratic Republic of Congo (DRC), atrocities against women have been so horrific and extensive that the violence has been referred to colloquially as the "war within a war" and the "war against women."[14] Although a peace process was initiated at the end of 2002, the prevailing lawlessness in the eastern part of the country continues to put many women and girls at risk. In research from 2005 in South Kivu, 492 women – 79 percent of whom had been sexually assaulted by between two and 20 attackers – shared their experiences of rape, mutilation and torture.[15] One incident was related by a woman who was still confined to a hospital bed:

"A few moments after the Interhamwe [Rwandan militia] arrived in the village, I heard my neighbour screaming. I looked out of the window and I saw some men, all holding rifles. Immediately, I wanted to run away and hide but three of them turned up at our house. My husband pretended to be asleep...they grabbed me roughly. One of them restrained me, while another took my pili pili pestle and pushed it several times into my vagina, as if he was pounding. This agony seemed to be a never-ending hell [...]

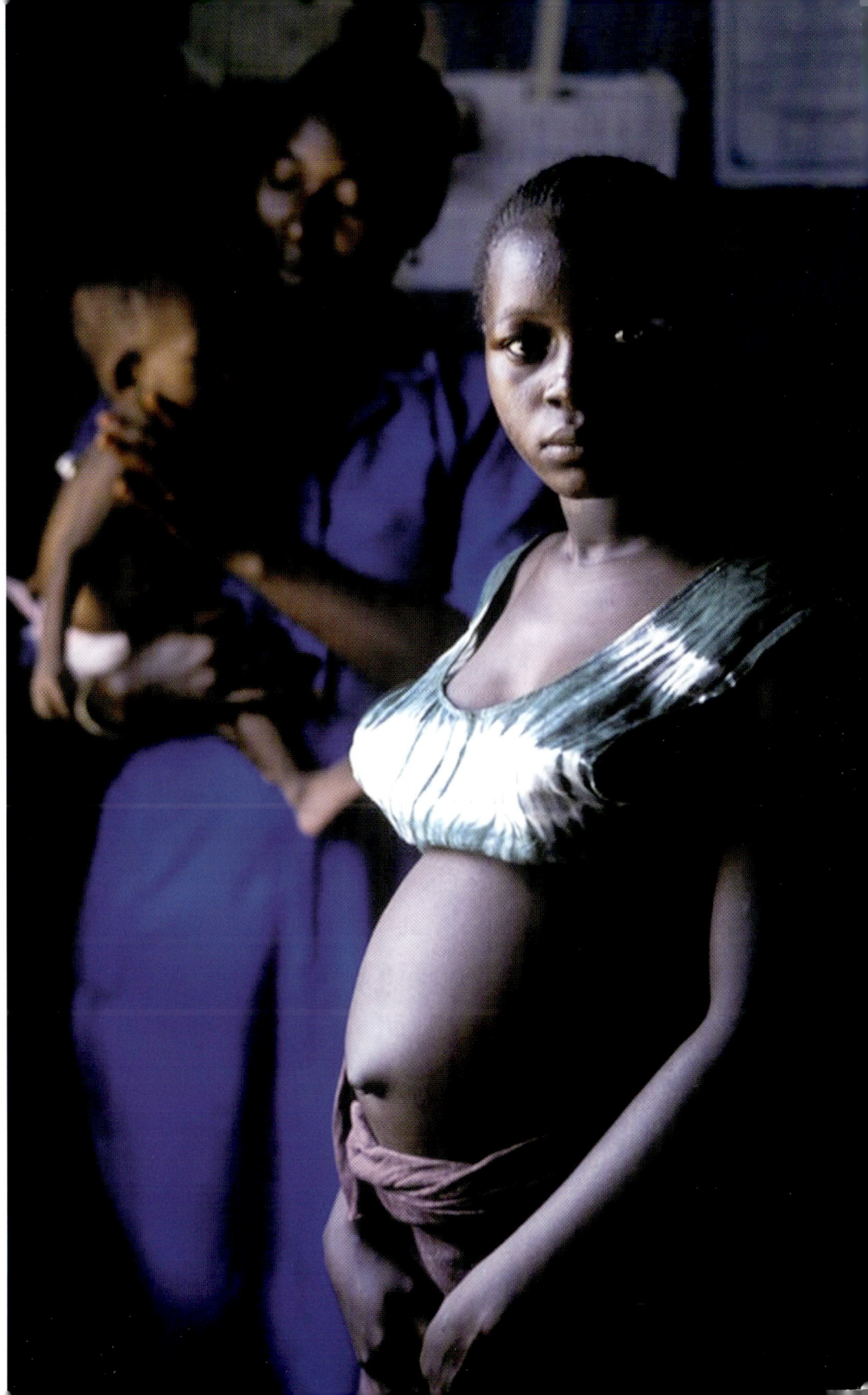

A 13-year-old girl and former "bush wife" who became pregnant through rape in Sierra Leone. She was fortunate enough to return to her family after peace accords were signed, but shortly afterwards her father threw her out of the household for bringing "dishonour" to the family. In the countless stories of this nature, the perpetrators are never brought to account for acts that shatter women's and girls' lives. In many cases victims suffer the secondary impact of rejection by their families and communities. Frequently, girls in this predicament find that prostitution is their only means of survival.

Image: Brent Stirton

A mother in Darfur, western Sudan, looks down at her newborn son – the child of a rape she survived in 2004. Rape in Darfur has been a common weapon of the Janjawid militia. Women and girls have been assaulted in their villages while searching for firewood outside camps for the displaced and even inside neighbouring Chad. The rapists commit their crimes in a climate of complete impunity, while their victims often suffer the additional indignity of marginalisation by society and, at times, their own families.

then they suddenly left. For two weeks my vagina was discharging. I was operated on …I have to relieve myself into a bag tied to an opening in the side of my belly. They also killed my husband and my son."[16]

… they grabbed me roughly. One of them restrained me, while another took my *pili pili* pestle and pushed it several times into my vagina, as if he was pounding. This agony seemed to be a never-ending hell …

In another instance, a Congolese woman described the brutality she endured at the hands of militia:

"I was busy cutting wood, when four armed men suddenly appeared at the other end of the field. They told me to undress and to volunteer myself to one of them. I refused. Then they took me, spreading my legs out and tying them, one to the bottom of a tree, the other to another tree trunk. They stuck my head between two sticks held diagonally, so that I couldn't sit up without hurting myself. I stayed in this position and one of the attackers penetrated me forcefully from behind in the vagina, and the other pushed his penis into my mouth, right into my throat … I was retrieved by some neighbours who watched my ordeal from a distance. When they found me I had fainted and was covered in blood."[17]

Similar atrocities were committed by all parties to Sierra Leone's 10-year civil war. The primary perpetrators of the most egregious abuses, however, were among the rebel forces, particularly the Revolutionary United Front (RUF). They raped as a matter of course, often in gangs, often in front of family members. They forced boys and men to rape their mothers and wives. They sexually assaulted and then disembowelled pregnant women. They mutilated women's genitals with knives, burning wood and gun barrels.

One particularly violent rebel incursion on the capital city of Freetown in January 1999 let loose a "hellish cycle of rape, sexual assault and mutilation."[18] A 13-year-old girl, abducted during the incursion and forced into sexual slavery by rebels, already had given birth to a baby girl born of rape by the time she told her story to researchers in 2001. She remembered how her captivity began:

"We were taken to a house with about 200 people in it. My older cousin was sent to go and select 25 men and 25 women to have their hands chopped off. Then she was told to cut off the first man's hand. She refused to do it, saying she was afraid. I was then told to do it. I said I'd never done such a thing before and that I was afraid. We were told to sit on the side and watch. So we sat. They chopped off two men's hands. My cousin couldn't watch and bowed her head down to avoid the sight. Because she did that, they shot her in the foot. They bandaged her foot and then forced her to walk. We left the two men whose hands had been cut off behind. We were then taken to a mosque in Kissy. They killed everyone in there. … They were snatching babies and infants from their mother's arms and tossing them in the air. The babies would free-fall to their deaths. At other times they would also chop them from the back of their heads to kill them, you know, like you do when you slaughter chickens. One girl with us tried to escape. They made her take off her slippers and give them to me and then killed her. […] One time we came across two pregnant women. They tied the women down with their legs eagle-spread and took a sharpened stick and jabbed them inside their wombs until the babies came out on the stick."[19]

The "murderous madness" of sexual violence in conflict

The motivation for rape committed during armed conflict varies. The violence can be a by-product of the collapse in social and moral order that accompanies war. In DRC, rape has become so indiscriminate as to be referred to as "murderous madness."[20] In one example, a Congolese mother walked into her house to find a paramilitary raping her 10-month-old baby.[21] Such incidents are not only limited to combatants. Men from the local community may exploit the chaos of conflict to commit sexual violence against women without fear of punishment. Under the volatile and disorganized rule of the Mujahideen, for instance, rape and sexual assault in Afghanistan's capital city of Kabul were reportedly so commonplace that the oppressive police state established after the Taliban takeover in1996 was initially perceived by some women as a welcome reprieve.[22]

Sexual violence may also be systematic, carried out by fighting forces for the explicit purpose of destabilising populations and destroying bonds within communities and families. In these instances, rape is often a public act, aimed to maximise humiliation and shame. In Timor Leste, Indonesian military reportedly raped women in front of their families and forced Timorese men to rape Timorese women. Researchers on a 2004 fact-finding mission to northern Uganda, where an 20-year insurgency by the Lord's Resistance Army (LRA) remains unresolved – despite the current peace talks, spoke with one man who was commanded by members of the LRA to have sex with his daughter: "I refused. … They ordered my son …

for the fear of a cocked gun he complied. ... I was then forced to have sex with a hole they had dug in the floor using a knife. ...They forced my private part in the hole several times – the skin was totally destroyed. ... It was impossible to fight someone who is armed. ...This was all done in front of my wife, son, and the daughter. ...My wife went mad."[23] A Sudanese man recounted to researchers his family's similar degradation in Darfur: "In February 2004, I abandoned my house because of the conflict. I met six Arabs in the bush. I wanted to take my spear and defend my family, but they threatened me with a weapon and I had to stop. The six men raped my daughter, who is 25 years old, in front of me, my wife and young children."[24]

Sexual violence also can serve to quell resistance by instilling fear in local communities or in opposing armed groups. In such cases, women's bodies are "used as an envelope to send messages to the perceived enemy."[25] In the Shan Province of Burma, where the government has been trying to violently suppress a local rebellion since the mid-1990s, hundreds of women have been systematically raped.[26] In one example, an army major approached a young girl and "asked her about her parent's [whereabouts] and ordered his soldiers to wait at the edge of the farm and arrest anyone who came to the farm. He then raped [the girl] in a hut several times during the day and at about 4 a.m. burned [her alive] in the hut, and left the place with his troops."[27] Comparable violations by Russian soldiers in Chechnya have been reported during "mop-up" operations that ensue after rebel Chechen fighters have decamped a town. Of four Chechen women vaginally and orally assaulted by Russian

of genitals and intentional HIV transmission are other techniques of ethnic cleansing. Women in Rwanda were taunted by their genocidal rapists, who promised to infect them with HIV. In Bosnia, Muslim women impregnated by Serbs reportedly were held captive until late term to prevent them from aborting.[30] In Kosovo, an estimated 100 babies conceived in rape were born in January 2000 alone – the International Committee of the Red Cross speculated at the time that the real number of rape-related pregnancies was likely to be much higher.[31] Sometimes attacks on women's bodies – particularly their reproductive capacity – specifically target perceived rival progeny. One woman from Darfur reported in 2004, "I was with another woman, Aziza, aged 18, who had her stomach slit on the night we were abducted. She was pregnant and was killed and they said, 'It is the child of an enemy.' " [32]

Sexual slaves to armed combatants

Many other instances have been identified where women and girls are abducted for the purposes of supplying combatants with sexual services. According to one soldier from DRC, "Our combatants don't get paid. Therefore they can't use prostitutes. If we politely ask women to come with us, they are not going to accept. So, we have to make them obey us so we can get what we want."[33] An elderly victim from Liberia, thought to be around 80 years old at the time she related her story to investigators, acknowledged being held by rebels in the town of Voinjama, where "at night, the men would come, usually more than one. They would rape me. They said they would help me. If I was lucky, they gave me 10 Liberian dollars (US 20 cents)."[34]

Particularly in conflicts defined by racial, ethnic, religious and other divisions, violence may be used to advance the goal of ethnic cleansing. Public rapes in Bosnia, for example, were used to instigate the flight or expulsion of entire Muslim communities.

More often the victims of sexual slavery are younger, and in many cases their victimisation comes under the terms of military duty. An estimated 40 percent of child soldiers around the world are girls, the majority of whom are forcibly or coercively conscripted.[35] Their responsibilities may range from serving as porters or participating in active combat, with the additional expectation that they will provide sexual services to their superiors or fellow combatants. Much of the violence reportedly committed against women and girls by guerrilla groups in Colombia, for example, is in the context of forced recruitment.[36]

military in February 2000, one purportedly suffocated to death while a soldier sat on her head.[28] In Colombia, paramilitary control of some regions often includes sexual violence and torture of women and girls. Intimidation campaigns are carried out on their bodies, as in one of many cases reported in 2001 to the UN Special Rapporteur on Violence Against Women, where a Colombian girl was raped and killed, her eyes and nails then removed, and her breasts cut off.[29]

Particularly in conflicts defined by racial, ethnic, religious and other divisions, violence may be used to advance the goal of ethnic cleansing. Public rapes in Bosnia, for example, were used to instigate the flight or expulsion of entire Muslim communities. Forced impregnation, mutilation

Even those women and girls who "voluntarily" join fighting forces are unlikely to anticipate the extent to which they will suffer sexual exploitation. Data collected in 2004 from women participating in

The decomposing bodies of a woman and girl, victims of the 1994 genocide in Rwanda.

"... if you looked, you could see the evidence, even in the whitened skeletons. The legs bent and apart. A broken bottle, a rough branch, even a knife between them. Where the bodies were fresh, we saw what must have been semen pooled on and near the dead women and girls. There was always a lot of blood. Some male corpses had their genitals cut off, but many women and young girls had their breasts chopped off and their genitals crudely cut apart. They died in a position of total vulnerability, flat on their backs, with their legs bent and knees wide apart. It was the expressions on their dead faces that assaulted me the most, a frieze of shock, pain and humiliation. For many years after I came back home, I banished the memories of those faces from my mind, but they have come back, all too clearly." (Excerpted from Shake Hands with the Devil, by Lt Gen Roméo Dallaire, Force Commander of the United Nations Assistance Mission to Rwanda, 1993-1994.)

Image: Mariella Furrer

Bosnian government troops reach out towards a Muslim woman who sits mute with shock by a roadside in Travnick, central Bosnia, in the summer of 1993. The woman was part of a group of Muslim detainees held captive by Bosnian Serbs. They had been deported across the frontline to the government-controlled area only minutes before this photograph was taken. Detainees who were with her said she had been raped.

Image: Anthony Lloyd

Liberia's disarmament and demobilisation programme indicate that 73 percent of the women and girls experienced some form of sexual violence.[37] In Uganda, a former child soldier of the National Resistance Army remembers: "We collected firewood; we carried weapons. For girls it was worse because … we were girlfriends to many different officers. … At the end it became, like, I don't own my own body, it's their body. It was so hard to stay the 24 hours a day thinking, which officer am I going to sleep with today?"[38] In a similar account from a 19-year-old woman voluntarily associated with the Maoists in Nepal, "Sometimes we are forced to satisfy about a dozen [militia] per night. When I had gone to another region for party work, I had to have sex with seven militia, and this was the worst day of my life."[39]

Some girls who are forced or coerced into sexual slavery may succeed in escaping their captors only to be seized again. Such was the experience of 16-year-old "Hawa", from Sierra Leone: "There were about 20 men. We ran to the bush, but I got separated from my family. I was with other people from the village, and we were captured by the rebels and taken to Liberia. … At first I refused to be a 'wife', but I had to agree because there was nobody to speak up for me, and nobody gave me food except the rebels. I was a wife for about eight months. … I had not even started my periods." Hawa eventually escaped and walked for three days in the bush until she got to a town where she found her parents. When they returned together to their remote village, Hawa recalled, "It was very sad when I … met my sisters because I felt I was somehow discriminated against because I had been raped." Two years later, Hawa was captured again: "It was a different group: This time I was always with them at night as their wife."[40]

Hawa escaped a second time and was reunited with her family. For too many other women and girls who attempt to escape the perils of war, the threat of sexual violence follows them – from flight, to displacement in camps or other settings, through to their return and resettlement in their home communities.

"Sometimes we are forced to satisfy about a dozen [militia] per night. When I had gone to another region for party work, I had to have sex with seven militia and this was the worst day of my life."

Flight

The UN High Commissioner for Refugees (UNHCR) estimated the total number of people displaced by armed conflict at the start of 2006 at 32 million: 8.4 million were refugees in neighbouring states, and another 23.7 million were internally displaced in their home countries.[41] According to the then UN Secretary-General Kofi Annan, "The differential impact of armed conflict and the specific vulnerabilities of women can be seen in all phases of displacement."[42]

During flight, women and girls remain at high risk for sexual violence – committed by bandits, insurgency groups, military and border guards. Many women must flee without the added safeguard of male relatives or community members, further increasing their vulnerability. In the case of 17-year-old Tatiana from the DRC, the results were devastating:

Tatiana was eight-and-a-half-months pregnant when her husband and her two-year-old son were hacked to death by irregular/rogue militia in May 2003. When she, her mother and two younger sisters heard that the same militia intended to raid the district of Bunia, where they lived, they fled. Six days later, they reached a militia checkpoint, but her mother could not pay the US $100 demanded. The militia cut her throat, killing her. When Tatiana's 14-year-old sister began to cry, she was shot in the head. Her other sister, age 12, was taken to a nearby clearing and gang-raped. Tatiana was told to leave at once or suffer the same fate. After six days walking, she went into labour and gave birth to a girl. Although she had lost a lot of blood, she had to take to the road again the following day. The baby later died.[43]

Without money or other resources, displaced women and girls may be compelled to submit to sex in return for safe passage, food, shelter or other resources.[44] Some may head towards urban settings, possibly in search of the relative security of a densely populated area or in the hope of obtaining employment. Whatever the motivation, both internally displaced and refugee women and girls in urban settings are at risk of exploitation by local residents, especially because they are less likely than encamped populations to be targeted for assistance and protection by governments or by humanitarian agencies.

Afghan refugee women living in the city of Peshawar, Pakistan, for example, described being forced to exchange sex for rent-free housing.[45] In Colombia, the Ministry for Social Protection reported in 2003 that 36 percent of internally displaced women in the country had been forced by men into sexual relations. This statement was later confirmed in a study undertaken in the same year, which found that displaced women living in barrios in or near Cartagena had suffered higher levels of physical and sexual violence after their displacement.[46] Unaccompanied girls are likely among the most vulnerable to sexual exploitation. A 1999 government survey of more than 2,000 prostitutes in Sierra Leone found that 37 percent of the young women were under the age of 15, and that the majority of them had been displaced by conflict and were unaccompanied by family.[47]

Still others attempting to escape from war may be the target of traffickers. The absence of border controls and normal policing make conflict-affected countries prime routes for traffickers. In Colombia, the ongoing internal conflict has given rise to one of the Western hemisphere's most active trafficking networks. Colombia's Department of Security estimated that 35,000 to 50,000 women and girls were trafficked in 2000, the majority to countries in Asia and Western Europe, as well as to the United States.[48] Myanmar, also wracked by long-standing civil conflict, is thought to supply some 40,000 trafficked women and girls annually for work in brothels, factories and as domestic labourers in Thailand.[49]

Displacement to camp settings

Camps for internally displaced persons or refugees may offer only limited protection from sexual violence. Humanitarian aid workers have consistently identified the danger to women who must venture outside the confines of camps to search for firewood or other staples unavailable in the camp. Research among refugees living in camps in Dadaab, Kenya, undertaken almost 10 years ago, found that more than 90 percent of reported rapes occurred under these circumstances.[50] Despite the long-standing evidence, not enough has been done to anticipate and avert this predictable risk in more recently established camps. One 27-year-old Liberian woman who had been raped twice before seeking safety in a camp for internally displaced persons (IDPs) described the circumstances of her third rape, in 2003, when she left the camp to look for firewood:

"There were three government soldiers with guns. One of them saw me and asked, "Where are you going?" I said I was looking for wood. Then he told me, You are assigned to me for the day. I was very afraid. He forced me to go far into the bush, and he undressed me. Then he raped me. When I got dressed afterwards, he took 50 Liberian dollars from me. [...] My stomach is very painful, but I don't have any money to go for treatment."[51]

The trend continues for encamped women displaced by the conflict in Darfur, Sudan, but in this instance, repeated reports of attacks by a

number of international human rights organisations resulted in recent efforts to improve policing and security related to firewood collection.[52] For many women, however, these security measures have come too late. Agencies continue to report high levels of rape despite the global publicity of the crisis and the presence of more than 7,000 African Union monitoring troops in Darfur since 2006.

Women are also at risk of rape in or near camps, particularly when the camps are poorly planned and/or administered. In a 1996 survey of Burundian refugee women displaced to a camp in Tanzania, more than one in four reported being raped during the prior three years of conflict, with two-thirds of the rapes occurring since displacement, either inside or close to the camp. The majority of perpetrators were other refugees (59 percent), followed by local Burundian residents (24 percent), and

> A 1999 government survey of more than 2,000 prostitutes in Sierra Leone found that 37 percent of the young women were under the age of 15, and that the majority of them had been displaced by conflict and were unaccompanied by family.

then local Tanzanians, soldiers and police.[53] As with firewood collection, advocates and humanitarians have for several years spoken out about the relationship between ill-considered camp design and violence against women, and have put forth recommendations for reducing women's vulnerability.

Nevertheless, the problem persists in many settings. A risk assessment carried out in 2004 in seven camps for the displaced in Montserrado County in Liberia concluded that overcrowded conditions, insufficient lighting at night, the close proximity of male and female latrines and bathhouses, and poor or unequal access to resources all conspired to increase the likelihood of sexual violence against women and girls.[54] In a 2004 study undertaken in northern Uganda, a woman living in one of many camps in the region told investigators, "Rape is rampant here ... a woman was recently harassed by two men who held her legs wide open and used a flashlight to observe her private parts and allowed another man to rape her while they observed."[55]

Lack of institutional protection

Not unlike rape in war, these acts of violence flourish in the environments of impunity that too often circumscribe the lives of displaced populations. The problem can be especially dire for displaced

A Sudanese refugee who was shot in the shoulder and leg as he defended his
daughters against the Janjawid militiamen who were trying to rape them. The
militiamen later tortured him by tying a cord around his testicles and pulling on it.
The ubiquity of rape as a weapon of war places enormous strain on male family
members, who are often helpless to prevent such assaults.
Photographed in Goungour, Chad, in 2004.

Image: Francesco Zizola/Magnum

Former abductees – some of whom spent years as forced labourers and "wives" for the Lord's Resistance Army in northern Uganda – relax in the Gusco Rehabilitation Centre. One girl holds a baby while another reads a newspaper with the headline, "Love: Don't force it. Don't rush it. Don't hurt it."

people. Despite the fact that in 1998 the UN produced guiding principles on the protection of displaced populations, there is still no UN agency specifically mandated with their care and protection. UNHCR is increasingly stepping in to fill the void, but in 2004 the refugee agency assisted only 5.6 million of the estimated 25 million internally displaced persons around the world. [56] This figure was still being used on their international website in February 2007. More often, the responsibility falls primarily to national governments, whose resources are likely to be drained or diverted by the conflict. A global evaluation of the reproductive health of refugees and IDPs by an interagency working group found that reproductive health services are most lacking among IDP populations, of which services addressing gender-based violence are the least developed.

The scenario may be only marginally improved for refugees. In too many instances, there is not enough UNHCR staff on the ground who are designated to address the issue of gender-based violence. Even where staffing is sufficient, UNHCR's ability to provide sustained protection against sexual violence is all too often only as good as a host country's commitment to addressing the issue. Wherever a host government or local community is hostile, the risk of all forms of violence against refugees – including sexual violence – is higher.

Following a statement issued in 2000 by the president of Guinea, for example, in which Liberian and Sierra Leonean refugees were blamed for sheltering armed rebels responsible for attacks on Guinea, women and girl refugees reportedly were raped in mob reprisals launched by Guinean police, soldiers and civilians.[57] Some 50 Burundian refugee women in Tanzania were allegedly attacked in May 1999 by a group of more than 100 Tanzanian men who were apparently avenging the death of a local schoolteacher.[58] Thousands of Afghans in Pakistan and Burmese in Thailand have never been granted official refugee status by their host governments. The fear of forced return means that they are unlikely to ever report a case of sexual violence committed against them to local authorities. Not surprisingly, in both Pakistan and Thailand multiple incidents have been recounted by refugee women of local police or security colluding in or even perpetrating sexual violence against them.[59]

What is perhaps more surprising is the extent to which humanitarian actors – those whose commitment is to provide assistance – have been implicated in sexual crimes against refugees and the displaced. A 2002 report jointly published by Save the Children-UK and UNHCR documented allegations against 67 individuals working in 40 aid agencies serving refugees in three countries in West Africa. One young refugee mother told researchers, "I have to sleep with so many men to

> What is perhaps more surprising is the extent to which humanitarian actors — those whose commitment is to provide assistance — have been implicated in sexual crimes against refugees and internally displaced persons.

make 1,500 GNF (37 US cents) so that I can feed myself and my child. [The locals] pay me 300 (7 cents) each time, but if I am lucky and I get [an aid] worker, he can pay me 1,500." Another refugee said, "In this community, no one can access CSB [a soy nutrient] without having sex first." [60] Although a UN-sponsored investigative team following up on the allegations questioned the verity of the report, multiple subsequent incidents of sexual exploitation by aid workers in camps in Kenya, Zimbabwe and Nepal, among others, has continued to draw attention to the seriousness of the problem. [61] In 2006 fresh allegations emerged of continued sexual exploitation of children by aid workers in a new Save the Children-UK investigation in Liberia.

Reconstruction or exploitation?

Evidence suggests that sexual violence does not necessarily end with the cessation of armed conflict. Incidents of rape are reported to have increased sharply in the context of ongoing insecurity in Iraq, for example. One of the victims, "Dalal", was abducted, held overnight and allegedly raped in 2003 by four Iraqi men whom she believes "wanted to kidnap anyone … to take what they wanted."[62] The US-based Human Rights Watch reported in July 2003 that at least 400 women and girls as young as eight years old had been raped during or immediately after the war. Underreporting due to the stigma against victims of sexual violence likely means that the real figure was much higher.

In other post-conflict settings, incidents of rape may decrease, but risk of exposure to forced or coerced prostitution, as well as trafficking, may increase. Events in the Balkans – where prostitution and trafficking burgeoned in the aftermath of wars in the former Yugoslavia – illustrate how criminal elements may replace fighting factions in the continued sexual victimisation of women and girls. The added presence of peacekeeping forces, who have been implicated as users of commercial sex workers in places such as Bosnia-Herzegovina, Sierra Leone,

Kosovo, Timor Leste and the DRC, may comprise a notable portion of local demand.

In many instances, the risk to women and girls of falling prey to sexual exploiters is exacerbated by reconstruction programmes that fail to specifically target their needs, or to address longstanding patriarchal traditions that discriminate against women. After the genocide in Rwanda, for example, inheritance laws barred surviving women and girls from accessing the property of their dead male family members unless they had been explicitly named as beneficiaries. As a result, thousands of women were left with no legal claim to their homes and land. Such impoverished women, returning to their communities without family or resources, are more likely to be caught up in the sex trade.[63]

Ironically, and sadly, women and girls who experienced sexual violence during conflict are probably the most vulnerable of all to further exploitation in post-conflict settings. Some rape victims may be rejected by their families and communities for having "lost their value."[64] In Burundi, women who had been raped told researchers in 2003 that "they had been mocked, humiliated and rejected by women relatives, classmates, friends and neighbours because of the abuse they had suffered."[65] Raped women may be abandoned by husbands who fear contracting HIV, or who simply cannot tolerate the shadow of

"Armed conflicts ... increasingly serve as vectors for the HIV/AIDS pandemic, which follows closely on the heels of armed troops and in the corridors of conflict."

"dishonour" they believe their raped wives have cast upon them. Without prospects for the future, prostitution may seem the only viable option to these women.

For other women and girls, their histories of victimisation may dull them to the dangers of entering the sex trade. One young girl in Sierra Leone who had been abducted by rebels voluntarily became a prostitute after she was released by her captors. She reportedly "considered herself fortunate that she was now being paid."[66] In Rwanda, an HIV-positive woman in Kigali told of a sister's resignation: "After the war, we saw our family decimated ... my little sister for whom I care is a pseudo-prostitute because she has no money. She says that she will continue this lifestyle even if she becomes HIV-positive. She says she looks at my health degrading and insists that she wants to taste life before she dies."[67] Disregard for one's own wellbeing is only one of the many

potential devastating effects of sexual violence on its survivors.

The impact on the survivor

Sexual violence against women in war and its aftermath can have almost inestimable short and long-term negative health consequences. As a result of the systematic and exceptionally violent gang rape of thousands of Congolese women and girls, doctors in the DRC are now classifying vaginal destruction as a crime of combat. Many of the victims suffer from traumatic fistula – tissue tears in the vagina, bladder and rectum.[68] Additional long-term medical complications for survivors may include uterine prolapse (the descent of the uterus into the vagina or beyond) and other serious injuries to the reproductive system, such as infertility, or complications associated with miscarriages and self-induced abortions.[69] Rape victims are also at high risk for sexually transmitted infections. Health clinics in Monrovia, Liberia, reported in 2003 that all female patients – most of whom said they had been raped by former government soldiers or armed opposition – tested positive for at least one sexually transmitted infection.[70] Untreated, these infections can cause infertility – a dire consequence for women and girls in cultures where their value is linked to reproduction. They also increase the risk of HIV transmission.

HIV/AIDS is among the most devastating physical health consequences – as evidenced by the continued suffering of women in Rwanda. In a study of more than 1,000 genocide widows undertaken in the year 2000, 67 percent of rape survivors were HIV-positive. In the same year, the UN Secretary-General concluded, "Armed conflicts ... increasingly serve as vectors for the HIV/AIDS pandemic, which follows closely on the heels of armed troops and in the corridors of conflict."[71] Despite the level of recognition of the urgency of the problem of HIV in war, insufficient resources have been dedicated to addressing the issue. In Rwanda, as elsewhere, treatment for rape victims infected with HIV has been characterised as "too little, too late."[72] The story of one HIV-positive victim of the genocide illustrates the tragic consequences:

"Since I learned I was infected [in 1999], my husband said he couldn't live with me. He divorced me and left me with three children, so now I don't know how to pay for food, rent, school and so on. I have no family left. My six-year-old has many health problems, and she must have HIV. She should be on antiretrovirals, but there isn't the money. Since I was married

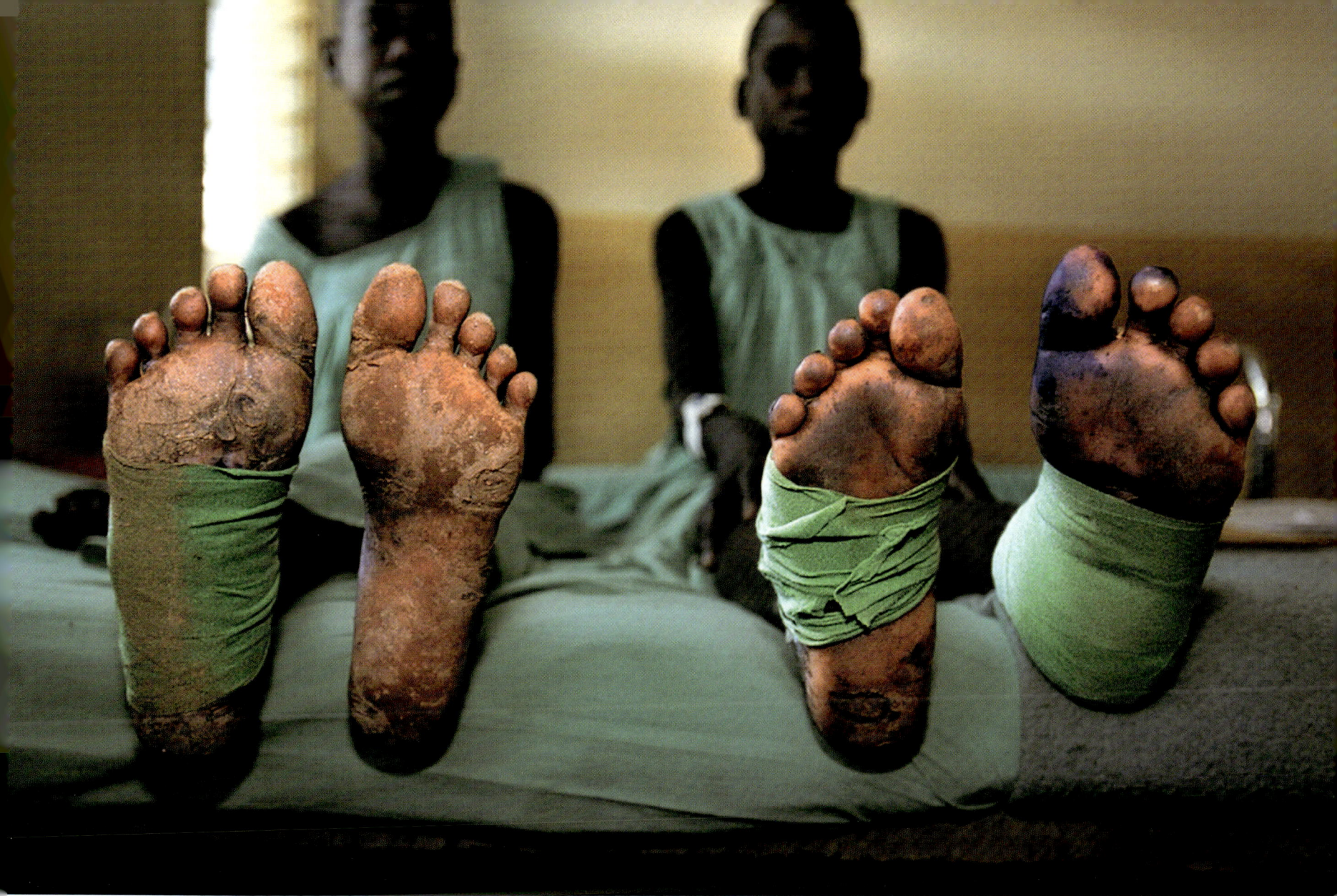

Recently liberated girls who were forced to work as porters and domestic slaves for the Lord's Resistance Army in northern Uganda awaiting treatment for their injured feet at St Joseph's Hospital in Kitgum. They were among the tens of thousands of children who were **abducted** and made to serve the rebels. During the two-decade conflict, young girls and women were vulnerable to physical and sexual abuse, not only at the hands of the rebels but by government soldiers as well.

Image: Sven Torfinn/OCHA

A group of sex workers in Freetown, Sierra Leone. Many of these girls were displaced from their villages by civil conflict and fled to the capital, where for lack of any other means to support themselves, they were forced to work as prostitutes. Girls displaced by war and thousands of others were raped, sexually enslaved and used as combatants and "bush wives" in different militia groups during the years of war. With little training or education and frequently with children, these women find it difficult to reintegrate into their communities.

after the war, it is difficult for me to access help from the Genocide Survivor's Fund. My greatest worry is what will happen to my children if I die. I want to get sponsors for them, so at least I can die in peace."[73]

The challenges of meeting the myriad health needs of survivors of war-related sexual assault are complicated by the absence of adequate facilities and trained staff in many war-torn settings. In research

"I regret that I'm alive because I've lost my lust for life. We survivors are broken-hearted. We live in a situation which overwhelms us. Our wounds become deeper every day. We are constantly in mourning."

conducted in post-conflict Timor-Leste and Kosovo, and among internally displaced women in Colombia, more than two-thirds of women interviewed reported that reproductive-health services were difficult to access.[74] Even where services do exist, they may not be free – as is the case in many countries in Africa, where state-run health centres operate on a cost-recovery basis. Moreover, many health clinics are constructed with open waiting areas where women are girls may be expected to disclose their reasons for seeking care; in the absence of confidentiality, they are likely to conceal their victimisation. Health workers' beliefs that it is their responsibility to "prove or disprove" rape is also a limiting factor in quality of care. In some settings, a woman seeking medical treatment may be required first to report her case to the police in order to get a medical referral. This prerequisite, in turn, may expose women to further violence.

Rape victims in Darfur, for example, have been arrested for "illegal" pregnancies (occurring outside the context of marriage). One 16-year-old Sudanese girl, who had already suffered the rejection of her family and fiancé, endured additional abuse at the hands of police:

"When I was eight months pregnant from the rape, the police came to my hut and forced me with their guns to go to the police station. They asked me questions, so I told them that I had been raped. They told me that as I was not married, I will deliver this baby illegally. They beat me with a whip on the chest and back and put me in jail. There were other women in jail who had the same story. During the day, we had to walk to the well four times a day to get the policemen water, clean and cook for them. At night, I was in a small cell with 23 other women. I had no other food than what I could find during my work during the day. And the only water was what I drank at the well. I stayed 10 days in jail and now I have to pay the fine – 20,000 Sudanese dinar [$65] they asked me.

My child is now two months old."[75]

For those who are subject to discrimination by family and community, and who also do not receive basic psychological support, the emotional effects of their violation may be as debilitating as any physical injuries. Many rape survivors in Rwanda reportedly "still live under a constant shadow of pain or discomfort which reduces their capacity to work, look after and provide for their families."[76] One such survivor, who was gang raped and beaten unconscious during the genocide, woke up only to witness the killing of people all around her. Ten years later, she says:

"I regret that I didn't die that day. Those men and women who died are now at peace, whereas I am still here to suffer even more. I'm handicapped in the true sense of the word. I don't know how to explain it. I regret that I'm alive because I've lost my lust for life. We survivors are broken-hearted. We live in a situation which overwhelms us. Our wounds become deeper every day. We are constantly in mourning."[77]

The implications of such testimony make clear that programming to assist survivors is imperative to any lasting efforts at reconstructing the lives and livelihoods of individuals, families and communities in the wake of armed conflict. In most conflict-affected settings, however, human rights and humanitarian activists are still fighting to ensure that the most basic services are accessible. The ultimate goal – putting an end to the epidemic of sexual violence against women and girls during war – seems an even more distant aspiration than developing adequate response services.

Assisting and protecting survivors

International humanitarian initiatives aimed at addressing violence against women in refugee, internally displaced and post-conflict settings are relatively new. Most have been introduced only in the last 10 years. Particularly during the late 1990s, a number of relatively small-scale but nonetheless vital projects were implemented in various sites around the world. The lessons learned from these efforts gave rise to a theoretical model, currently promoted by UNHCR and others, that recognises the importance of integrating prevention and response programming within and across service-delivery sectors, specifically in the areas of health, social welfare, security and justice.[78] In other words, survivors must have access to medical care as well as psychosocial assistance; they should be able to rely on the protection of the police, peacekeepers and local military; and they are entitled to legal assistance should they choose to prosecute those who perpetrate violence against them. Addressing sexual violence also requires national education and sensitisation – at the family and community level and at the level of service provision – so that doctors, lawyers, judges and police are able to respond to survivors efficiently, effectively and supportively. It further requires advocating for improved legislation to protect women and girls, as well as policies that support gender equity and equality.

While the broad outline of roles and responsibilities within this "multisectoral model" provides a general framework for addressing violence against women, an assessment undertaken in 2001 concluded that the implementation of the model was weak in virtually every conflict-affected setting around the world.[79] Foremost among the limitations to establishing multisectoral programming was the failure – at both the international and national levels – to prioritise violence against women as a major health and human rights concern. The result was a lack of financial, technical and logistical resources necessary to tackle the issue. Many survivors, the 2001 assessment observed, were not receiving the assistance they needed and deserved, nor was sufficient attention being given to the prevention of violence. The outcomes of an independent experts' investigation spearheaded by the UN Development Fund for Women the following year echoed these

violence against women and girls. Widespread community-based education aimed at changing attitudes and behaviours that promote sexual and other forms of violence against women has been carried out in a number of settings. Research on the nature and scope of the problem has also multiplied in recent years, and is bringing pressure to bear on international actors as well as on states to take more aggressive measures to address violence against women in conflict and its aftermath.

In addition, several high-level international initiatives are currently underway to promote more coordinated and comprehensive action by humanitarian aid organisations. New guidelines issued by a task force of the UN Inter Agency Standing Committee (IASC) provide detailed recommendations for the minimum response required to address sexual violence in emergencies and hold all humanitarian actors responsible for tackling the issue in their respective areas of operation. The IASC released a statement in January 2005 reconfirming their commitment to "urgent and concerted action aimed at preventing gender-based violence, including in particular sexual violence, ensuring appropriate care and follow-up for victims/survivors, and working towards holding perpetrators accountable."[81]

To this end, a global initiative to "stop rape in war" is being developed collaboratively by UN entities and nongovernmental agencies. Two major pillars of the initiative include conducting advocacy at the international, regional and local levels, and strengthening

...the last decade has produced significant advances in international standards and mechanisms of accountability for those who commit sexual violence.

findings in their conclusion "that the standards of protection for women affected by conflict are glaring in their inadequacy, as is the international response."[80]

These inadequacies persist even today. However, the number of field-based initiatives addressing the issue of sexual violence against women and girls continues to grow, even against a wearisome backdrop of limited funding. Methodologies are being refined by many humanitarian organisations to try and extend and improve services for survivors, and well as to build the capacity of local organisations to take on the issue. Standardised procedures for medical management of rape are being adopted in an increasing number of settings. Training modules have been developed to build local capacity to meet the psychosocial needs of survivors. Efforts are being made, most evidently in post-conflict settings but also in some refugee settings, to support legal reforms that would provide greater protection against multiple types of gender-based

programming efforts among those currently engaged in addressing the issue of sexual violence in conflict. One of the notable outcomes of the proposed initiative is to reduce the prevalence of rape in the target countries by at least 50 percent by 2007. Such ambitions will require a "quantum shift" in approaches to sexual violence in war, most especially in terms of prioritising all efforts to end the levels of impunity that have given rise to the "shocking scale and stubborn persistence" of the violence.[82]

The final frontier: ending impunity

Along with an increase in field-based programming, the last decade has produced significant advances in international standards and mechanisms of accountability for those who commit sexual violence. International criminal tribunals for Rwanda and the former Yugoslavia have prosecuted sexual violence as crimes of genocide, torture, crimes

Girls chat together in the dormitory of the Gusco Rehabilitation Centre in northern Uganda. Most of the former abductees at the facility were virtual slaves to the rebel Lord's Resistance Army (LRA) and forced into sexual relationships with its soldiers. Cecilia (not pictured here), aged 20, was abducted from a secondary school in Pader when she was 15 and spent five years in captivity. She is now at a rehabilitation centre in Kitgum.

"I was given to John Okech, one of [LRA leader Joseph] Kony's senior commanders. I was his fourth wife. He soon brought in four other young girls. They were to become his wives when they were slightly older. In the meantime, they were told to baby-sit for his other wives. When you are given a commander as your husband, you're expected to produce food. You're also given a gun and expected to fight. I was often picked to go out on patrols.

I became pregnant in early 2002, when Kony predicted an attack from the UPDF [United People's Defence Forces] on our bases in Sudan. By June, our whole group sneaked back into Uganda and hid in the Imatong Mountains. This was the most difficult time for captives. My husband was part of the attack on Anaka [a village in Gulu District]. He was shot in the chest by the UPDF. He died a few days later. I gave birth to a baby boy, but he died after a month.

I was released after my husband died. I only returned from the bush a few days ago. I'm still haunted by frightful dreams. I dream only that I'm still in the bush. I hear children crying. I dream that we are being attacked, or fighting, walking for days in the hot desert without food or water. I'm happy to be back, but I have no hope of returning to school. I heard that my entire family was displaced. They are scattered in camps in the district."

[Excerpted from *"When the sun sets, we start to worry …"* An account of life in northern Uganda published by the UN Office for the Coordination of Humanitarian Affairs (OCHA)/ Integrated Regional Information Network (IRIN) in 2003.]
Image: Sven Torfinn/OCHA

"Carolina" grew up on a farm in the northern province of Sucre, Colombia. When armed militia terrorised her village in 2001, Carolina and her family were forced to flee. They relocated to Nelson Mandela, a ramshackle *barrio* for internally displaced persons on the outskirts of the port city of Cartagena. Carolina, then 14, was often left alone to watch her younger siblings while her mother worked. She was seduced by a neighbour in his sixties, who wooed her with pocket money and treats. He raped her three times over a period of several months. Carolina told her parents about the rapes only after she realised that she was pregnant, having previously feared the neighbour's threat to kill her family if she told them anything. With her family's support, she reported the rapes to the authorities — who declined to investigate. With the help of a lawyer, Carolina is currently seeking justice through the Inter-American Commission on Human Rights in Washington, D.C.

against humanity and as war crimes. The Rome Statute of the recently established International Criminal Court (ICC) has enumerated rape, sexual slavery and trafficking, enforced prostitution, forced pregnancy, enforced sterilisation and other forms of sexual violence and persecution as crimes against humanity and as war crimes. The ICC is initiating investigation into cases from several conflict-affected countries.

Another groundbreaking advance was the UN Security Council's adoption of Resolution 1325 in 2000, which specifically "calls upon all parties to armed conflict to take special measures to protect women and girls from gender-based violence, particularly rape and other forms of sexual abuse, and all other forms of violence in situations of armed conflict."[83] Since that time, the UN Secretary-General has submitted two reports to the UN Security Council on the implementation of Resolution 1325. While these reports concede that much remains to be done, especially in terms of holding states accountable for the actions of fighting forces and in increasing the level of participation of women in all stages of peace-building, they also note that major advances have been made in introducing codes of conduct that establish "zero tolerance" for all UN personnel, including peacekeepers, who might sexually exploit those they are meant to serve. Since these codes of conduct were implemented, action has been taken against offenders in a number of countries, from Timor Leste, the Middle East and Africa to Kosovo and Haiti. U.N. Assistant Secretary-General for Peacekeeping Jane Holl Lute said in January 2007 that the U.N. has done more in the last two years than ever before to try to combat sex abuse in its 16 peacekeeping missions. Between January 2004 and the end of November 2006, Lute said, the UN investigated allegations of sexual exploitation and abuse involving 319 peacekeeping personnel "in all missions".

However, grave problems with impunity persist in virtually every conflict-affected setting around the globe. International tribunals can only prosecute a fraction of cases, and many national governments do not have the resources or the commitment to pursue the perpetrators of sexual crimes against women. In some cases national jurisdiction does not extend to foreign fighting forces who commit abuses within their territory. In others, governments do little to support victims in coming forward. Evidentiary requirements often mean that the burden of proof lies with the victim. Some must pay for legal assistance. Where forensic evidence is required, healthcare providers must be able to collect it in a timely manner and be prepared to present that evidence at a trial. Police or relevant security forces must be trained to investigate and appropriately document their findings. The frustrating reality for many survivors of sexual crimes in conflict-affected settings around the world is that there are no systems to ensure basic protection to survivors, let alone access to justice.

Such impunity both reflects and reinforces the widespread cultural norms that acquiesce to the inevitability of violence against women and girls whether in times of peace or of war. And it is these norms that must be targeted aggressively in order to ensure reductions in levels of abuse: "In a world where sex crimes are too often regarded as misdemeanours during times of law and order, surely rape will not be perceived as a high crime during war, when all the rules of human interaction are turned on their heads, and heinous acts regularly earn their perpetrators commendation. ... What matters most is that we combine the new acknowledgement of rape's role in war with a further recognition: humankind's level of tolerance for sexual violence is not established by

> grave problems with impunity persist in virtually every conflict-affected setting around the globe. International tribunals can only prosecute a fraction of cases, and many national governments do not have the resources or the commitment to pursue sexual crimes against women.

international tribunals after war. That baseline is established by societies, in times of peace. The rules of war can never really change as long as violent aggression against women is tolerated in everyday life."[84]

In a world where thousands of women suffer sexual violence committed with impunity in the context of conflict, the message needs to be made clear: A single rape constitutes a war crime. ■

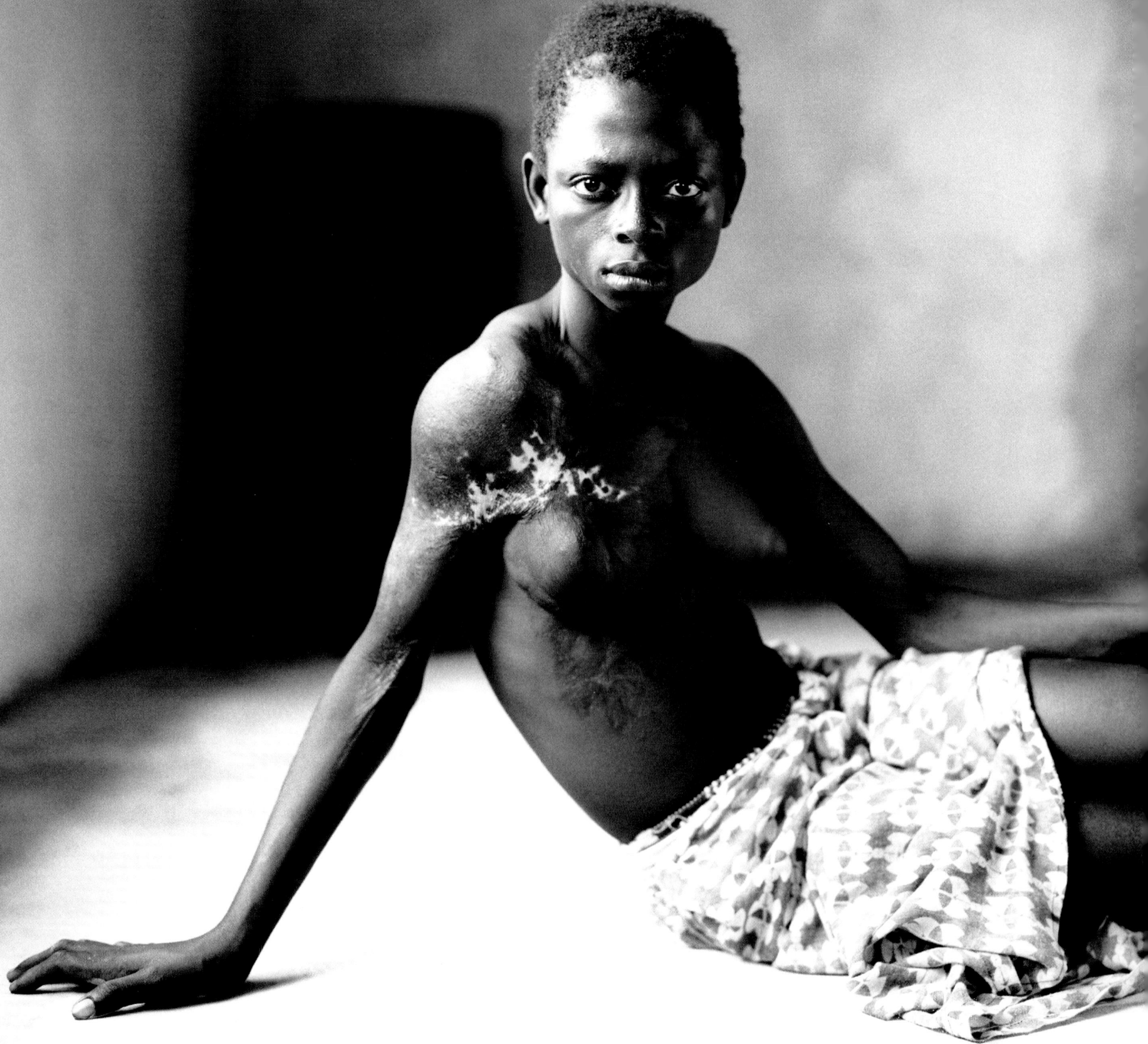

A young former "bush wife" in Sierra Leone, who was abducted from her family at age 10 by rebels from the Revolutionary United Front. After a killing spree that decimated most of her village, the rebels took her away with them to work as a cook, porter and sex slave. When she tried to escape, the rebels poured acid over her arm and breast as a warning to other abductees. After two years in captivity, she was able to escape. She recently joined a small self-help group of female torture victims. Sierra Leone has only one psychologist, and there are thousands of female victims of sexual abuse and torture — who have no choice but to help themselves.

Francoise is 16 years old and at the time of this interview had been living for three months at SOS Grand Lacs, an, outreach programme in Goma, Democratic Republic of Congo (DRC). She was abducted from her village in northeastern DRC by Interhamwe soldiers, members of a Rwandan militia group.

"I was born in a village near Bukavu. There were 11 children in my family, but two died from illness. I am the third-born. I never went to school. We didn't have an easy life; before we were able to eat we had to cultivate land for other people.

In September 2004, I was taken from my home. It was night time, around 2 a.m., and the Interhamwe attacked our village. They came to our house after visiting my uncle's. He worked for Pharmakina [a drug company in Bukavu], and they looted his house, taking his money, his good clothes, his good dishes. Two Interhamwe broke open the door to our house and forced their way in. They asked for money and we told them we had nothing. They asked us for our clothes, but when they saw they were worthless they left them. They left my family alone and took me. My family couldn't put up a fight, as they knew they would be killed. The soldiers made me carry all the things they had looted from my uncle's house. On the way to their base in the bush, they raped me. They took off my clothes, and as one held me down the other raped me, then they swapped. I said to them, Now you have raped me — can I go? They said no and if I continued to insist they would kill me.

The place they live in the bush is far from civilians. It was like a big football pitch, with groups living in tents. They had dug trenches, to use when other military attack. The Interhamwe live on all they loot. It was very cold there. We rarely saw the sun because of all the trees. I was taken as the wife of the two men who abducted me. They told me, You will be our wife. If you die, you will die here. I stayed in the tent with these two men, but I slept on the leaves that covered the floor. Whenever we heard guns from attackers, we ran. They ran into the trenches, but I wasn't allowed to go in. I just had to run until I found a bush to hide in.

There were other girls there, but I can't remember how many. Sometimes I heard the Interhamwe talking about raping people in the villages. They spoke with pride. I was never allowed to talk to anyone. I did all the ordinary things a woman does: cooking, sweeping, washing clothes. I was never given a gun. Sometimes I had to work in the vegetable garden. These two men were adults; I don't know their exact age. They forced me to have sex with them every day, whenever they wanted, sometimes four or five times a day. They never used a condom, but I never got pregnant. I sometimes have a yellowish discharge with blood. I have been given treatment by DOCS [Doctors On Call Services, a nongovernmental agency that provides medical help and counselling]. It isn't better yet.

They would attack villages in turn, one group one week then another the next. If they looted things that could be sold, they would go to a local market, in civilian clothes, and sell them. I overheard them saying this was the best life possible for them, because if they went back to their country they would not be accepted.

One day I tried to escape. I took a route I didn't think would be used, but I met some Interhamwe on the way. They beat me so hard, using sticks. They also sliced my leg near the ankle with a machete — you could see the bone. I was given no treatment. The wound just festered until I managed to escape. I just kept thinking God would help me escape these people.

One Thursday, when a group had gone to sell things they had looted and the others were in the garden, I decided to escape along the same route that brought me here. I left in the morning. At about 11 a.m., I passed some girls looking for wood. I explained my situation, and they took me to their families. They said there had been other girls who were abducted, but they hadn't come back. When I started to tell my story I felt so terrible. The people I was staying with must have told a pastor. He came to me and said that because I was so sick he would take me to his place in Minova. He took me there from Kalonge, and I stayed with him for one month. A lady came to me and told me she would take me to Goma. She looked after me for four days, and it was through her friend at the general hospital that I was taken to Unicef and then bought here.

Sometimes I dream about the Interhamwe coming here to kill me. When I have this dream, the next day is a very bad day. When I was being held by the Interhamwe, I heard them say: We will never leave Congo. Our aim is to torment other people's lives."

Pornographic magazines belonging to American soldiers in Iraq being burned as rubbish, 2006. Experience suggests that most battle-hardened and/or brutalised soldiers, removed from access to the usual outlets for sexual frustration, are potential rapists and therefore must be controlled. Even when rape is not part of a particular military strategy, rape tends to be more common amongst armies/armed groups that lack discipline or operate in small numbers, with more independence and lower accountability to command structures.

Image: Brent Stirton

perpetrators and motivation:
behind rape and sexual violence in war

In Iraq, Human Rights Watch reported in July 2003 that at least 400 women and girls as young as age eight had been raped during or immediately after the war. Underreporting due to the stigma against victims of sexual violence likely means that the real figure is much higher.
In a survey of Rwandan women in 1999, 39 percent reported being raped during the 1994 genocide, and 72 percent said they knew someone who had been raped.
"In the eastern Congo, over 12,000 rapes of women and girls have been reported in the last six months alone." – Under-Secretary General for Peacekeeping Jean-Marie Guéhenno, October 2006
Of a sample of 410 internally displaced Colombian women in Cartagena who were surveyed in 2003, 8 percent reported some form of sexual violence prior to being displaced, and 11 percent said they had been abused since their displacement.

Rape and sexual violence by armed and uniformed, state and non-state forces, as well as civilians, is the greatest direct threat to civilian women during conflict. Of all the abuses committed in war, rape is one specifically inflicted against women. Despite increasing evidence that a number of men are sexually abused and raped during conflict, it is the women and girls who are still the unacknowledged casualties of the world's conflicts, which currently rage in 35 countries, from Iraq and Chechnya to Colombia and Sudan.

Rape in war has been such a common occurrence throughout history that it has attracted little attention or analysis. Indeed, women were – and in certain conflicts still are – viewed by combatants as legitimate spoils of war. It has been tolerated precisely because it is so commonplace. Only relatively recently has the motivation behind rape in war and its prevalence been documented and explained, predominantly by human rights groups seeking to end the impunity that accompanies these abuses.

A better understanding of these particular violations is being pursued through extensive documentation and testimony from past and ongoing conflicts of the last 25 years in countries including Bosnia, Bangladesh, Peru, Rwanda, Vietnam, Burma, the Democratic Republic of Congo (DRC), Chechnya, Iraq, Liberia, Sierra Leone, Sri Lanka, Colombia, Sudan and northern Uganda. Such is the shame of rape for most women, and the fact that many women are killed after being raped, that the world will never know the true extent of sexual violence or the number of rapes suffered by the victims of armed and uniformed men.

Despite its pervasiveness, rape is often a hidden element of war. Because the abuse is largely gender-specific and committed by men against women, it is usually narrowly portrayed as being sexual or personal in nature, as a "private crime" or a sexual act. Rape, however, is sometimes part of a premeditated political or military strategy. Ignoring the fact that sexual violence against women and girls is used as a combat tactic trivialises what in reality is a war crime.

Increasingly, human rights activists are pushing for a more accurate understanding of the political function of wartime rape and the complexity of its motivation in order to develop adequate and responsive remedies.[1] In 2007, a campaign called Stop Rape in War will be launched and include activities to promote more active participation by men's groups, who can

In fact, rape in war routinely serves a strategic function and acts as an integral tool for achieving particular military objectives.

contribute to the campaign as well as add to the understanding of motivation. Although these efforts are crucial to enhancing accountability for wartime rape, some commentators have warned they also risk isolating sexual assault from other forms of violent physical or psychological abuse against either women or men during conflict.

Sociopolitical motivations

A United Nations human rights report on rape and sexual violence from 1998 echoed the growing view that sexual attacks were motivated by political and social factors. "This overall deterioration of the condition of women in armed conflict situations is due not only to the collapse of social restraints and the general mayhem that armed conflict causes, but also in many cases to a deliberate and strategic decision on the part of combatants to intimidate and destroy 'the enemy' as a whole by raping and enslaving women who are identified as members of the opposition group."[2]

Organised rape can be used as a strategic device to accomplish particular political and social ends. In fact, rape in war routinely serves a strategic function and acts as an integral tool for achieving particular military objectives. It may be used to intimidate or punish individual women and social groups, to destabilise and demoralise communities or to drive unwanted people from their land.[3] Conflicts in the last decade in the Balkans, the ongoing atrocities in Darfur, western Sudan, in Burma, and the mass rape of women and girls during the 1994 genocide in Rwanda are examples of rape being used to achieve these kinds of ends. In certain cases, such as Rwanda, rape was used as a form of ethnic cleansing: Women were raped by men from a rival ethnic group, and thus, in a culture where ethnicity is determined by paternity, bore children of that

opposing ethnic community. In Sudan today, agencies have received reports of "Arab" rapists telling their "African" women victims, We will make you a lighter baby – another example of ethnic cleansing or manipulation.

According to reports from Africa Rights, a human rights organisation based in the United Kingdom, Rwanda may stand as the paradigmatic example of "genocidal rape," owing to the fact that many of the Tutsi women who were gang-raped have subsequently tested positive for HIV. Tests conducted on the 25,000 Tutsi women members of the Widows of Genocide (Avega) organisation showed that "two-thirds were found to be HIV-positive. ... Soon there will be tens of thousands of children who have lost their fathers to the machete and their mothers to AIDS."[4]

In northern Uganda, during the 20-year civil conflict between the government and the rebel Lord's Resistance Army(LRA), some women complained that the Ugandan army was deliberately bringing in HIV-positive soldiers to rape and abuse the Acholi people.The Acholi are those Ugandans indigenous to the rebel area who have often accused the central government of neglect or marginalisation. There may be more inferred, rather than hard, evidence that HIV-positive soldiers intentionally raped women to infect them with HIV. Instead, it may more realistically be an indicator of the fact that HIV prevalence is high in African military organisations because of lack of services and high-risk behaviour. Rape can be a factor in HIV exposure – certainly, violent rapes can cause an even higher rate of transference due to tissue tearing.

According to reports by Human Rights Watch, sexual violence in the Sierra Leone conflict was extraordinarily brutal and frequently preceded or followed by violent acts against victims' family members. The rebel factions used sexual violence to terrorise, humiliate, punish and ultimately force the civilian population into submission. [5] This was also the case in Liberia.[6]

Sexual violence is often marked by the systematic breaking of taboos and undermining of cultural values. Rape of women in war almost always occurs in connection with other forms of violence or abuse against women or their families and violations of international humanitarian law. Men may be forced at gunpoint to rape female family members or other men as a means to terrorise and humiliate people. Researchers argue that it is important to place rape in this context in order to understand that it is, as are other wartime assaults, a human

Members of the rebel Sudanese Liberation Front in West Darfur. As the conflict between the Sudanese government, irregular Janjawid militia and different antigovernment rebel forces drags on, the number of reported rapes continues to rise. While initially most of the reports identified the Janjawid as the main perpetrators, rebel forces, local police and other security personnel are also alleged to be involved.

Image: Thomas Grabka

Armed men in Iraq, 2006. The violence of the situation in Iraq has created chaotic civil-war conditions as sectarian groups, extremists, Ba'athist loyalists and criminal gangs face off against each other, the new government, the foreign forces and the civilian population. Iraqi women have spoken about their increased vulnerability in a setting where traditional cultural taboos have broken down and rape and kidnapping of women and girls has become more common.

Image: Brent Stirton

rights abuse. Moreover, "the harm inflicted by rape may be compounded by other concurrent violations against either the rape victim or those close to her."[7] In many cases, this may be entirely intentional.

The perpetrators in these cases frequently act with the tacit or explicit approval of their political or military leaders. While many rapists in these contexts may claim, after the event, that they were coerced into committing rape, there is a long history of rape being seen and enjoyed as the spoils of war – "carnal booty" as some have described it.

Something often overlooked in reports on wartime rape is a distinction, if not legal at least academic, between war crimes committed in the heat of battle – for example, the shooting of enemy soldiers trying to surrender – and crimes committed afterwards or before. A distinction is necessary because the mental state of people in combat is categorised by some as almost a form of madness, during which they are not entirely responsible for their actions and during which more extreme brutality may be found. [8]

Many testimonies from survivors of sexual violence during war describe the men as under the influence of drugs or alcohol. The use of alcohol prior to battle has a long history. According to historical records, British forces during the battles of Agincourt, Waterloo and the Somme were given generous amounts of brandy, the suggestion being that alcohol or other stimulants limit fear while the increased adrenaline caused by battle removes the detrimental physical aspects of subsequent drunkenness. The anonymous author of A Woman in Berlin wrote about the Nazis leaving behind stores of alcohol for the advancing Soviet forces and reasoned that "only a man would not realize that this would cause the numbers of rapes to go up."[9]

Reports of wartime rape from the Balkans, West Africa, northern Uganda and DRC are full of such examples. Intoxication reduces inhibitions, impairs reasoning and judgment, distorts contact with reality and decreases sensitivity to the impact of one's behaviour on others. However, researchers agree that alcohol is not what causes a man to commit rape. While alcohol may be a catalyst and play a contributing role, it is not causative. Alcohol and drugs, it appears, act as "releaser" when an individual has already reached a frame of mind in which he is prone to rape.

This section seeks to explore the motivation that drives perpetrators to commit acts of gender-based violence against women. Many writers and commentators describe the behaviour of perpetrators in different ways, using sociological, cultural or psychological constructs, but some of the individual testimonies researched for this section and for the earlier IRIN publication, Broken Bodies Broken Dreams – violence against women exposed, were so gratuitously brutal and so utterly careless of the suffering of the victim that the term "evil" seems to be the only suitable description.[10]

> While alcohol may be a catalyst and play a contributing role, it is not causative. Alcohol and drugs, it appears, act as 'releasers' when an individual has already reached a frame of mind in which he is prone to rape.

The roots of combatant behaviour in war

In 2005, the International Committee of the Red Cross published a study on the Roots of Behaviour in War in order to better understand different violations of international humanitarian law (IHL), including sexual violence. They focused on the particular conditions men find themselves in physically and psychologically when part of an armed group in conflict. The following four factors are significant catalysts to enable individual men to commit atrocities and were considered as relevant to this discussion on the motivation to rape:

Group conformity. Combatants are subject to group conformity phenomena such as depersonalisation, loss of independence and a high degree of conformity. This is a situation that favours the dilution of the individual responsibility of the combatant within the collective responsibility of his combat unit. It also leads to a culture of silence and resistance when facing any accusations from outsiders against the behaviour of one or more members of the group.

Obedience to authority. Combatants are also subject to a process of shifting individual responsibility from themselves to their superior(s) in the chain of command. While violations of IHL may sometimes stem from orders given by such an authority, they seem more frequently to be connected with a lack of any specific orders not to violate the law or an implicit authorisation to behave in a reprehensible manner. There are examples in DRC that suggest militia commanders give their men days off with full licence to rape and pillage at will. In a recent well-publicised case, four US soldiers were accused of raping and killing a 14-year-old girl in Iraq. Details of the case suggested discipline had broken down in their group and the commanding officers were generally ignorant of their soldiers' behaviour.

The spiral of violence. Violations of IHL are not generally the work of sick, sadistic or irrational individuals. Combatants who have taken part in hostilities and been subjected to humiliation and trauma are prone, in the short term, to perpetrate violations of IHL. Often they are victims, or perceive themselves as victims, of violence as well. It has been reported that in Colombia and Guatemala conscripts were often forced to rape people – sometimes their own family members – as a means to break down their natural moral resistance and make them more capable of committing acts of brutality.

The progressive nature of moral disengagement. Moral disengagement is not only a gradual process but also one that determines behaviour that draws from past actions the force needed to sustain future actions. Psycho-sociologists have shown that group norms change progressively and that behaviour towards the victims evolves. What would once have been inconceivable becomes first acceptable and then normal.[11] In Men, Militarism, and UN Peacekeeping, the author argued that sexual exploitation and abuse started to become more acceptable in Somalia as Canadian troops lost faith in their reasons for deployment. They dehumanised the Somalis by calling them "skinnies" and gradually began to hate them, making it easier for them to act in ways they never would at home.[12]

It has been reported that in Colombia and Guatemala conscripts were often forced to rape people – sometimes their own family members – as a means to break down their natural moral resistance and make them more capable of committing acts of brutality.

An additional factor, often seen in Western armies, is the group machismo that evolves in close-knit combat units in which sexual as well as combat performance is highly prized, similar in manner to sports teams. During the first and second conflicts in Iraq, US troops were frequently shown violent pornography by their superiors to increase their aggression. Cases of gang rape by Western troops seem to have been strongly influenced by group pressure.[13]

Combat motivation studies suggest that a soldier's primary motivation is related to loyalty to his immediate comrades and a considerable fear of being shown up in front of them. Thus rape is also governed by the norms and values created by the military institution. For groups of testosterone-charged young men who have been removed from the constraints of normal society – and, importantly, who have already

made a huge psychological leap in which the greatest taboo of functional society, the killing of another human, is no longer taboo, but a point of pride and reward – the "lesser" crime rape becomes more acceptable.

Ideologies of rape

In the last quarter of a century, rape per se has occasioned intense ideological debate, not only within the legal system but within the feminist and human rights movements as well.

Recent attempts to prevent rape have been informed by the social science explanation of rape – also commonly referred to as the feminist theory of rape. This explanation holds that rape is an attempt by men to dominate and control women and that the motivation to rape has little, if anything, to do with sexual desire. It also contends that rape only occurs when males are taught by their culture, directly or indirectly, to rape. When adapted to explain rape in war or by uniformed groups this approach favours the explanation of rape in war as a weapon, tool, strategy or tactic. In some cases, such as the Balkan war and Darfur, western Sudan, there is strong evidence that it has been used as such.

Research studies that pre-empted the conclusion that rape in war is not principally a sexual act include those conducted in the 1970s by A. Nicholas Groth, a clinical psychologist and author of Men Who Rape: The Psychology of the Offender.[14] His research with rape offenders suggested that all sexual assault is an act of aggression, power or sadism regardless of the gender or age of the victim or the assailant. Neither sexual desire nor sexual deprivation is the primary motivating force behind sexual assault. It is not about sexual gratification, but rather a sexual aggressor using somebody else as a means of expressing their own power and control. His interpretation of his findings was that generally rape is a distortion of human sexuality. It is "sexuality in the service of nonsexual needs".

Groth categorises (peacetime) rapists into three groups: those whose primary motivation is power; those who are expressing and discharging anger and rage; and, finally, those who rape for sadistic reasons, where aggression and sexuality are fused. Perhaps, in the special conditions of war and conflict where armed men have extraordinary power over civilians, and where there is an expectation of impunity for their actions,

US forces in Iraq make deeply unpopular and regular incursions into private homes in search of enemy forces, insurgents and illegal arms caches. Formerly regarded as a disciplined force in a culturally sensitive and militarily hostile context, the US forces' reputation became badly tarnished by cases of sexual and physical abuse of prisoners and the rape and murder of a young Iraqi woman and three members of her family in March 2006 in Mahmoudiya.

Image: Brent Stirton

these three categories are redundant. In fact, they may merge together as uniformed men find themselves virtually unchallenged, unimpeded and even positively encouraged to indulge emotions of anger, power and sadism as well as sexual opportunism.

Evidence suggests that in war, in the thousands of varied cases of sexual violence, an unholy merger of these different emotions is at work. In many cases, it serves to express issues of mastery, strength, control, and authority (i.e., power rape). At the same time, sex is used as a weapon to defile, degrade and humiliate the victim where rape constitutes the ultimate expression of anger (i.e., anger rape). Anger rape, according to Groth, is also characterised by a disproportionate use of brutality to force a woman to comply with coerced intercourse.

Violent details of rape testimonies also often point to a sexual transformation of anger and power where aggression itself is eroticised. The rapist finds the intentional maltreatment of his victim intensely gratifying and takes pleasure in her torment, anguish, distress, helplessness, and suffering (i.e., sadistic rape). Sexual areas of the victim's body become a specific focus of injury or abuse. Hatred and control are eroticised, and rapists find satisfaction in abusing, degrading, humiliating and, in some cases, destroying their female captive. Their instrument is sex, but their motives are punishment and destruction, according to Groth and many subsequent analysts of contemporary rape.

However, there has been an absence of empirical research to date concerning the specific psychological motivations and causes of this behaviour by combatants. Most commentators lean on the current social science explanation to explain rape in war, shaping their theories on what they see as the traumatic social impact of wide-scale sexual abuse and working backwards to infer the source of motivation. This approach

"In some documented instances of rape, the abuse appears to serve not only strategic or political functions but also the perverse sexual gratification of the attacker …"

carries the danger of ascribing too narrow a reason for rape in war – as predominantly a tactical strategy or policy – while ignoring the possible additional individual, or collective, reasons that result in sexual violence by men in conflict scenarios. As one author wrote, "It is no longer politically correct to suggest that there may be as many motives for rape as there are for murder or other violent crimes."[15]

A more radical feminist analysis of rape places it as an inevitable expression of misogyny, which forms the foundation of patriarchal human society. For example, researchers on rape by US soldiers during the Vietnam War found that despite its rampancy, rape during the war received little critical attention by either the media or the military except in a small number of celebrated cases. It simply was not considered relevant or noteworthy for comment.

For some writers, this was not a case of sexual opportunism or sexual deprivation during battle but a failure to distinguish sexuality from gender by the military, the media and other observers. "The misogyny and devaluation of women which inform our cultural codes are reflective of a masculine dominated gender system. These attitudes toward women are not a product of essential or biological differences between men and women. Nor is misogyny an extension of male desire. […] Hence, acts of violence against women must be understood not as sexual crimes but as gendered crimes."[16] For writers ascribing to this view, the violations are an extension of masculine hegemony in everyday society, unleashed and permitted to run their course in war.[17]

While stressing the political or strategic use of rape in war, some analysts also admit that sexual opportunism and gratification plays a role. "In some documented instances of rape, the abuse appears to serve not only strategic or political functions but also the perverse sexual gratification of the attacker. Somali women refugees in Kenya typically are raped after being successfully robbed. […] The plights of 'young' and 'pretty' Burmese women kidnapped by soldiers and kept at army barracks for raping and of the thousands of women pressed into service as 'comfort women' during World War II further demonstrate that rape's function ostensibly may be not only to achieve overt political ends but also to satisfy the sexual proclivities of the attacker."[18] In Darfur today – where some claim rape has moved away from attacking and more towards sexual opportunism and harassment during firewood gathering – women often send out the old women or the very, very young to save the other women. The rapists, apparently, punish the old or young by "whipping or beating" them rather than raping them, indicating that suitability (from the rapist's perspective) is a criteria for rape and not just aggression. The Darfurian women certainly understand it as such and strategise accordingly.[19] To overlook the role of sexual opportunism in war runs the risk of offering an unbalanced perspective of central motivations for perpetrators.

The biological controversy

Generally, the "nurture" position rejects the idea that men have a natural propensity to violence or that men have "uncontrollable" violent and sexual urges. In the case of intimate-partner abuse, for example, observers point out that men are able to control themselves in settings where the social or professional cost of their behaviour would be too high, but are unwilling to exercise the same restraint behind closed doors. Equally, most men who rape in war are unlikely to do so in peace time.

Most researchers reject the notion that biology can be blamed for violent behaviour. Male violence, they say, is not genetically based but is instead perpetuated by a model of masculinity that permits and even encourages men to be aggressive. "Men's monopoly of violence stems from lifelong training in sexist models of masculinity."[20] Anthropological research has shown that domestic violence, for example, is virtually nonexistent in some particular societies, and therefore is not an inevitable human condition.[21]

Those advancing this perspective challenge apologists for male violence, who use biological arguments or the "psychopathological model" for male sexual violence to explain men's behaviour. Instead, they insist that these men are not "sick" or pathological and are responsible for their actions. They are men who behave reprehensibly, with free, conscious choice.[22]

The counterargument to this opinion claims that men, to some degree, are captive to their libidos and biology. This view maintains that the historic and global evidence of men's natural aggression and the biological imperative cannot be ignored. While socialisation may play an important role in how people behave in different societies and at different points in history, the "nature" position argues that sexual violence is too widespread and too overwhelmingly perpetrated by males to suggest that men and women are not motivated and driven by different forces.

In a controversial publication in 2000, two scientists went further in their challenge of the established social science explanation of rape. They argued that although a given rapist may have numerous motivations for committing a rape, social scientists have failed to prove that sex is not one of these. "Nor have social scientists seriously and honestly considered the vast evidence showing that rapists are sexually motivated."[23] In their book A Natural History of Rape, Thornhill and

Palmer suggest that sexual stimulation is a proximate cause of raping and is the common denominator across human rapes of all kinds. While defending their much-criticised work, they stated that although they agree that "culture (= social learning) plays a major role in the cause of rape, we challenge the notion that rape only occurs when males are taught by their cultures to rape. Rape not only appears to occur in all known cultures, but in a wide variety of other species where there is certainly no cultural encouragement of such behaviour."

Certain feminists have also supported the idea that the potential for rape is possibly more inherent to males than conventional and current ideologies of rape accept. In her book Sexual Personae, Camille Paglia offered a different ideological interpretation. Instead of viewing our culture or society as the cause of rape, Paglia argued that it is the main

> **Thornhill and Palmer propose the idea that in males the desire to rape pre-empts the permission or instruction to rape. They also suggest the driving force is predominantly sexual in origin.**

protection women have against attack. Thus, women can walk down a street unmolested not in spite of society, but because of its civilising impact on men. "Society is not the enemy, as feminism ignorantly claims. Society is woman's protection against rape."[24] Paglia, Thornhill and Palmer propose the idea that in males the desire to rape pre-empts the permission or instruction to rape. They also suggest the driving force is predominantly sexual in origin.

Power and sexual opportunism?

In violent conflict, with the disintegration of social structures, destruction of norms and accountability for antisocial behaviour, combatants are in fact unfettered by normal restraints and have the power to subject civilian women and girls to their demands. Irrespective of whether sexual violence also serves a function of political or strategic policies, the rampancy of rape in war suggests male sexual opportunism; driven by the male libido, may be a significant motivating factor.

Evidence supporting this notion includes numerous testimonies from conflict areas in the DRC, Uganda and Liberia, where women have been abducted and enslaved as "bush wives" to cook, clean and provide sexual services to single or groups of men. The women provide a utility through sex (forced) and work and are not necessarily brutalised, injured or killed despite the enforced conditions. In fact, many women affiliated

Young combatants in West Africa.
Reports from conflicts where child soldiers are used as combatants suggest that they are often the most brutal, violent killers and the most effective at terrorising civilians. Child soldiers are responsible for many acts of rape and sexual torture – sometimes against their own communities and/or family members. The recruitment of child soldiers is now considered a crime under international law and the Rome Statute of 1998. The issue, however, poses a difficult social and legal problem for those seeking to end impunity because of the age of the combatants and the circumstances of their recruitment, as the children are often coerced.

Images: Brent Stirton

with fighting forces are often the last to be released, if they are released at all, by militaries during the disarmament and demobilisation process (DDR) because of their value to the group. This leads their being left out of DDR processes and often has very negative ramifications for their reintegration into society, let alone the continued denial of their rights. In 2005, the US-based nongovernmental organisation Refugees International expressed its concern that the DDR process allowed former Interhamwe combatants in the DRC to repatriate their Congolese "bush wives" with them to Rwanda.[25]

In so far that the combatants can abduct new women to replace those they have tired of or those that may have died or escaped, these women

Once captured, victims often described trying to attach themselves to one rebel as a means to avoid gang rape, be given a degree of protection and be subjected to less hardship. They often became pregnant, had children and remained with the rebels for years.

are often considered expendable and manifestly objectified by their captors. This, however, is not always the case. In northern Uganda, the LRA second-in-command, Vincent Otti reportedly burnt down the village of an absconded "wife" and killed a number of people in his efforts to "recover" her.

New research suggests that the value of these "bush wives" and abductees to rebels and armed groups may have been underestimated. Dyan Mazurana has written about forced impregnation in northern Uganda that could make a case for the rebels' intention to hold sexual control over these young women and the value, to rebels, of children born in captivity.[26]

Most of the rapes during the civil war in Sierra Leone documented by Human Rights Watch occurred during attacks against a hamlet, village or town. During the course of the attack, the victims were most often abducted and forced to become sexual partners or "wives" to their rebel captors. Once captured, victims often described trying to attach themselves to one rebel as a means to avoid gang rape, to be given a degree of protection and be subjected to less hardship. They often became pregnant, had children and remained with the rebels for years.[27] This is also reminiscent of the anonymous diarist's accounts of Berlin at the end of the World War II, when women attached themselves to high-ranking Russian commanders to avoid gang rape.

Additionally, numerous testimonies indicate that younger and more

attractive women are often, but not always, at higher risk of rape. "The view that physical attractiveness influences risk factors is consistent with women at the ages of peak attractiveness (late teens and early twenties) being the most frequent victims of rape. Although the majority of rapes involve pubescent and young adult females, some rapes involve other victims."[28]

Discussing the prevalence and motivation for rape in Darfur, human rights worker Jane Lindrio Alao said, "They take the young ones – leave the old ones – and rape them. When we ask why they think these people did this, they'll say that during the actual rape, the man said that maybe he did it because she was a Fur. [a Darfurian ethnic group] [...] Sometimes because they accuse them of supporting rebels. Sometimes because they just want to."[29]

Women in flight from fighting or terror during conflict, whether in a camp for refugees or internally displaced people or when crossing international borders, often find themselves in situations where they are forced to trust certain authorities for their protection. These women are often vulnerable to sexual attacks by perpetrators who may be indifferent to the ethnic or political origins of the women under their care and simply abuse their power for sexual gratification.

A case involving the Bangladeshi Rohingyas community illustrates the plight facing countless women under the "care" of males in authority. The Burmese government maintained that the Rohingyas were illegal immigrants from Bangladesh and never belonged in Burma the first place. They forced more than 200,000 refugees into neighbouring Bangladesh. An October 1993 Human Rights Watch report detailed the abuse, including rape, of Burmese refugees by Bangladeshi military and paramilitary forces in charge of refugee camps.[30]

Equally in the DRC during the civil wars of the late 1990s, when different rebel groups and different national armies crisscrossed the eastern regions, countless women and girls were raped. Often women were raped numerous times by different passing armies in an atmosphere of what can only be described as predatory sexual opportunism rather than a systematic strategy to humiliate and victimise "enemy" civilian females.

A normal aspect of war?

In his recent book Berlin: The Downfall, historian Anthony Beevor highlighted the mass rapes carried out by the Soviet army during World War II. Beevor established that advancing Soviet troops raped large numbers of Russian and Polish women being held in concentration camps, Russian women who were returning to Russia during the advance on Berlin, as well as millions of German civilians – crimes for which they have become notorious.

The extent of the Red Army's "indiscipline and depravity" emerged as the author studied Soviet archives. He has since declared that details of the Soviet soldiers' behaviour have forced him to revise his view of human, specifically male, nature, whether the sexual violence was sanctioned at higher level or not. Having previously rejected the extremist's view that all men are potential rapists, Beevor said he was forced to conclude "that if there is a lack of army discipline, most men with a weapon, dehumanised by living through two or three years of war, do become potential rapists."

Beevor is careful to qualify any suggestion that what happened from 1944 onwards is in any way typical of male behaviour in peacetime. However, he considered that the indiscriminate nature of the rapes that continued during and after the end of the war in USSR-occupied areas "completely undermined the notion that the soldiers were using rape as a form of revenge against the Germans.

"By the time the Russians reached Berlin, soldiers were regarding women almost as carnal booty; they felt because they were liberating Europe they could behave as they pleased."[31] What is also interesting here is the different way in which women and children were treated by the Russian soldiers. There are numerous stories of the kindness of Russians towards small children that contrast dramatically with the horrific gang rapes of even old women in Beevor's book.[32]

The anonymous German journalist in Berlin, whose diary of spring 1945 was republished in 2005, described the Soviet raping spree following their takeover of the city. The Russians in A Woman in Berlin: Eight Weeks in the Conquered City clearly regarded sex as war booty, not as a weapon. Some even made gestures of courtship and offered remuneration for their pleasure.

The feminist Susan Brownmiller in her 1975 book Against Our Will documented how rape had been used as a weapon to destroy morale in all known wars. However, her study also suggested that gang rape is a normal aspect of war and men who rape in war are not psychopaths but ordinary men thrown into extraordinary, all-male circumstances.[33] It appears that like looting, rape is also a by-product of war – men who would not normally enter shops and private homes to take souvenirs and ship them home find themselves doing so – women almost seem to be seen as an extension of this, further objectified and not seen as human beings with rights but as property there for the taking.

"...that if there is a lack of army discipline, most men with a weapon, dehumanised by living through two or three years of war, do become potential rapists."

One writer researching rape by American soldiers during the Vietnam War found that raping Vietnamese women was, according to soldiers that were interviewed "standard operating procedure" for those on combat duty.[34]

Wartime rape has long been a question of discipline in armies. This is an assumption that most battle-hardened and/or brutalised soldiers, removed from access to the usual outlets for sexual frustration, are potential rapists and therefore have to be controlled. In the absence of a particular military strategy, rape tends to be more common amongst armies/armed groups that lack discipline or operate in small groups with more independence and lower accountability to command structures.

Interestingly, many armies until quite recently used officially sanctioned brothels, some of which travelled with the army. Even today, many Central and West African rebel groups have had their "bush wives"/sex slaves accompany them close to areas of combat. The German army in World War II used army brothels extensively, as did the Japanese, who enslaved and coerced more than 200,000 "comfort women" throughout different military stations in Asia.

The greater contemporary interest and awareness of rape in war may account for increased data on the scale and scope of the violations, but the nature of modern warfare is also a contributing factor. While classical interstate wars were capable of producing appalling levels of sexual violence throughout history, the newer predominance of intrastate warfare tends to be fought in and amongst the civilian population, therefore making rape or sexual violence (and other atrocities against civilians) more likely.

In many conflict settings, the deterioration of law and order and the breakdown of social structures allows those with guns to rule. Many victims of sexual violence around the world identify the threat of a gun, as opposed to another weapon or brute force, as the reason why they surrendered to their ordeal.

Images: Brent Stirton

Ideology serving causes

Different ideologies and explanations of rape serve different causes. For many activists seeking to stigmatise and outlaw rape in war, it is important to de-sexualise violations in order for them to be taken seriously as a war crimes, as crimes against humanity or even as human rights abuses. They resist the notion that biological differences between men and women may be the root cause of rape or that rape is primarily a sexual act, in part because it has not been proven and they fear it "trivialises" the crime and in part because it cannot be allowed to stand as an excuse for these crimes.

In human rights work, the assessment of motivation is crucial to determining the nature of the abuse and the remedy to be applied. Notwithstanding any natural proclivities males may have to violence

"…Decisive intervention on these social figures would spread confusion…, thus causing first of all fear and then panic, leading to a probable retreat from the territories involved in war activity."

and sexual predation it is seen as critical to establish rape in war as something that can be controlled, mitigated, legislated against and ultimately changed.

Sexual brutality against women and girls must no longer be seen as a tragic but inevitable outcome of war, argued a report by Amnesty International, which insisted insisting that rapes, torture and killings do not occur "naturally," but are a deliberate strategy of combat.[35] The report demanded an end to impunity for perpetrators – whether they are conventional soldiers, members of armed groups or peacekeepers. However, the legal distinction between armed groups and conventional soldiers becomes important, as the former are already to some extent beyond the law and the application of justice for a criminal act committed by somebody who is legally a criminal becomes somewhat problematic.

"This has to stop. We've had enough," said Hilary Fisher, director of Amnesty International's worldwide Stop Violence Against Women campaign. "In recent years, the assumption that justice is an unrealistic goal in conflict situations has been challenged. Prosecutions are the key."[36]

Taking such a stance not only conforms to current sociological explanations of rape, but practically assists activists to seize important legal territory. "Efforts to ensure that rape is prosecuted effectively by the International Tribunal established to try war crimes committed in

the former Yugoslavia have underscored the difficulties in applying international human rights and humanitarian law to rape. In order to overcome these difficulties and to end the appalling history of impunity for this abuse, rape in conflict must be understood as an abuse that targets women for political and strategic reasons."[37] In the case of Bosnia, the use of rape and sexual violence was very specific and systematically used as a political and terrorising tool by Serbian forces as they implemented ethnic cleansing in Bosnia.

The similarity of atrocities committed in town after town lends credence to Beverly Allen's assertion in her book Rape Warfare[38], that the strategy used by the Serbians against Muslims in particular was the result of specific analysis and debate. Allen quotes one document retrieved from the Serbian war planners that offers a chilling sociological rationale for the tactics of ethnic cleansing:

"Our analysis of the behaviour of the Muslim communities demonstrates that the morale, will, and bellicose nature of their groups can be undermined only if we aim our action at the point where the religious and social structure is most fragile. We refer to the women, especially adolescents, and to the children. Decisive intervention on these social figures would spread confusion […], thus causing first of all fear and then panic, leading to a probable retreat from the territories involved in war activity."

The paramilitary men who performed the rapes and effected ethnic cleansing therefore knew that they must be brutal enough, and inventive enough in their cruelty, that stories of their terror would quickly spread to the next village.[39]

Acts of violence against women may, therefore, be understood not as sexual crimes but also as gendered crimes with political intent. Many observers argue for the de-sexualisation of rape so that it can be seen for what it is: "a tragic consequence of political, economic, and social processes that generate and maintain domination over women in every cultural domain."[40]

Written over a decade ago, Thomas and Regan's work on rape in warfare echoes the determination of many activists and offers a conclusion to this article, "If we are to move forward in understanding rape as criminal behaviour and prosecuting it as such, then we have to represent it for what it is: a violent, gender motivated crime, a crime against women because they are women. As long as violence is linked to sexuality in representations of rape, the realm of sexual desire and its representations will also be distorted and misunderstood."[41]

While this analysis is important and serves to raise the status of rape as a serious crime there is a danger that this analysis is exaggerated. The view that rape is almost a symbolic act, related to power or politics, runs the danger of being overplayed, when it may also, often, be a release of sexual frustrations or snatching of sexual opportunism in abnormal situations. The analysis of why men rape at all should not be separated from what takes place in conflict.

A correct analysis of the causal motivation for sexual crimes is central to our efforts to combat them. If the explanation for different forms of gender-based violence in the world centres around sexist issues of male domination, patriarchal control, false senses of women's honour, discrimination and denial of equal human rights, it should not be surprising to see these same behavioural characteristics played out in war. – played out with more violence and less restraint in a context that is both more violent and less restraining than in times of peace.

The fight against HIV/AIDS in recent decades has shown that in order to design effective prevention and behaviour-change strategies, understanding sexual behaviour and social motivation is indispensable. Nothing is more "private" and covered in myth, denial and subject to

> **To assume that rape in warfare is always part of greater political policy or military strategy, to describe it as a "weapon of war" may not always be accurate or useful.**

denunciation than human sexual behaviour. If we want to end the scourge of rape in war and work to prevent gender-based violence, we must understand more about the perpetrators and what motivates them.

To assume that rape in warfare is always part of greater political policy or military strategy, to describe it as a "weapon of war" may not always be accurate or useful if, in fact, the reasons are deeper and more general and reflect more fundamental issues between men, women and human society. There may be as many motives for rape as there are for murder or other violent crimes, and the contemporary dominant view of rape as a strategy or weapon is not unchallenged. However, wartime rape may be the result of an intersection of dynamics, scenarios and situations, requiring an equally multifaceted understanding and response if it is to be punished, let alone ultimately curbed and reduced. ∎

"Marni " is 23 years old and has been a commercial sex worker in the Democratic Republic of Congo (DRC) since she was 14. Although she would like to find another means to earn a living, a lack of money, education and job opportunities has left her believing prostitution is "my only way". She currently lives with her three daughters in Goma, in northeastern DRC. She was raped by a group of men two days before this interview.

"I was born in the town of Bukavu. I was the third born in a family of nine – six boys and three girls. I went to school until the fourth form and then had to stop because we had no money. I was 11 years old when the Interhamwe [Rwandan militia who fled into neighbouring DRC following the 1994 genocide] came to Bukavu. It was at night. My father was asleep in my parents' room with my nine-year-old sister, and the rest of us were sleeping in the living room. My mother was still awake.

The Interhamwe came in the back door, so we were able to escape out the front. But my father and sister didn't manage to escape. I was so afraid. We ran through the night to the Rwandan border. We went through the bush, as it was too dangerous to go through the towns because of the militia. We slept outside at the border for two days, and then we went back home. The militia had taken everything and left the dead bodies of my father and sister. The men had raped her – the neighbours had heard her screaming, You are raping me! You are raping me!

There was nobody to help me. For three years, I sold fruit to make some money, but then I decided to become a prostitute. We had no food; I couldn't go to school – I had no other means. I went to stay with a friend who was doing the same. She was 19 years old. I stayed with her and she gave me food, but she also took all the money I earned. I was just 14. We shared a room, but when she had clients, I was sent into the living room with my client. I had to use a mat on the floor. We used to earn around [US] $2 to $4 per client. We worked day and night and received men of all ages.

We didn't use condoms – I didn't know about diseases then. I have been to a clinic and tested negative for HIV. I now insist the clients use condoms, unless it is a man I like, and then I don't. I lived with that girl for two years until one day a client gave me money to rent a small house. I would receive civilians and military [government soldiers], up to 10 clients a night. My friends told me about condoms, so I started using them.

There was not enough money in Bukavu, so I decided in September 2004 to visit my uncle in Goma. I wanted to start a small business and stop being a prostitute, but when I was chased away by my uncle's family I had no choice. I sold my clothes and my mobile phone and rented a room in Goma and started working as a prostitute. Life is good here in Goma because the money is good. I earn around $5 per client. I get all kinds of clients: civilians, government soldiers and MONUC [the United Nations peacekeeping mission in DRC]. I don't care who it is that comes; for me it is business. MONUC pay good money – up to $20.

I have do this work to pay for food and clothes to make me look nice so the clients like me. This is my only way. I have three daughters [ages seven, six and three] all from clients, I don't know who their fathers are. One client I have stays here every night, as his wife has gone off with another man. I have told my children he is their father. I don't love him; he pays me money, like all other clients, for sex. If I have other clients, he goes to the chair in the living room [she lives in a wooden hut with a tin roof]. My children don't know the reality of my work, as I send them out when a client comes. When they grow older I want to try and stop, because I don't want them to know. I would like them to go to school. I am afraid of this environment; it is not a good one for children. I dream to become a businesswoman, so I can build a house and don't

have to pay $12 per month for rent. If I get money I will give up this work. I want to stop prostitution. People are so afraid of diseases – I have been to the clinic once a month for the last three months.

The day before yesterday I was raped in Goma. I was looking for clients at Cap-Sud [a hotel] but hadn't found any and was on my way back home. It was midnight. Seven strong men forced me to the side of the road and raped me. I resisted, but it was not enough. They said, We will kill you if you don't accept. Then the military came and they ran away. I have had a pain in my stomach. I don't know what diseases they may have. I went to see a doctor and took medicine. It's getting a bit better now. I went to tell the military, and they said they would look for them. I don't know what has happened since."

A victim of rape in Bukavu, Democratic Republic of Congo (DRC). Although far less common than the rape of girls and women, there have been a substantial number of reports of male rape and sexual torture from different conflicts, including the DRC, Sierra Leone and Timor-Leste. This man left his family to search for food, and while doing so, he and three women were set upon by militia, who raped and killed the women. When they had finished, five men took it in turns to rape him. He remembers asking them, How is this possible? This is not something human beings do. Left for dead, he was saved by local forest people, who nursed him back to health.

Image: Brent Stirton

addressing impunity: sexual violence & international law

" The indictment charges [former Liberian President] Charles Taylor with 'bearing the greatest responsibility' for war crimes (murder, taking hostages); crimes against humanity (extermination, rape, murder, sexual slavery); and other serious violations of international humanitarian law (use of child soldiers) in Sierra Leone. The indictment against Taylor sends a strong message that no one is above the law when it comes to accountability for war crimes, crimes against humanity, and serious violations of international humanitarian law.

The statutes for the Rwanda and Yugoslav Tribunals and the International Criminal Court similarly bar immunity based on official position, reflecting the increasing trend by international courts to bring officials to justice for war crimes, crimes against humanity and violations of international humanitarian law, even while they are still in office. " (Excerpt from Human Rights Report, 4 June 2003.)

An unprecedented campaign

Widely known is the infamy of the Imperial Japanese Army, which between 1937 and 1945 forced some 200,000 girls and women into sexual slavery in different parts of Asia. In the early 1990s, numerous survivors broke their silence about this government-sanctioned network of sexual abuse. At first, the Japanese government denied having any evidence of "comfort station" operations, but following continued international pressure, it finally admitted in 1993 the military's role in organising slave brothels. It refused, however, to take direct responsibility and only helped to set up a private fund to financially assist the victims.

First proposed in early 1998, the Women's International War Crimes Tribunal on Japan's Military Sexual Slavery was held in Tokyo in December 2000. It was an extraordinary event — a people's tribunal —

organised by Asian women and human rights organisations and supported by international nongovernmental organisations. It was set up to adjudicate the Japanese military's sexual violence, in particular the enslavement of "comfort women"; to bring those responsible to justice; and to end the ongoing cycle of impunity for sexual violence against women during times of war.

Sixty-four survivors from nine countries and areas in the Asia-Pacific region took part in the tribunal. More than 1,000 people from throughout the world observed the proceedings, which were presided over by judges from the United States, Argentina, the United Kingdom and Kenya.

For the first three days, the tribunal heard the testimonies of survivors; scholars in history, international law, and psychology; and two Japanese veterans. In addition, the court received the voluminous evidence submitted by the nine country prosecution teams and two chief prosecutors. On 12 December, the fifth day of the proceedings, the tribunal issued its preliminary judgment, which found Emperor Hirohito guilty, and the State of Japan responsible, for the crimes of rape and sexual slavery as crimes against humanity.

Judge Gabrielle McDonald of the United States, former president of the International Criminal Tribunal for former Yugoslavia, read out the 50-

For many analysts and activists, the issue is the mischaracterisation of rape as a sexual crime against individual women and their honour, rather than as a violation of the victim's physical integrity and human rights.

page summary of findings. In addition to the verdict against Hirohito, the judges determined the government then "incurred state responsibility for its establishment and maintenance of the comfort system." The tribunal did not have authority to impose punishments, and Hirohito (1901-1989) and the other accused were already dead.

"We accomplished what the 1946-48 Tokyo Tribunal failed to do," stated tribunal organiser Yayori Matsui, referring to the post-war military tribunals held to judge Japanese war criminals while the Nuremburg courts were judging Nazi accused. To date, the response from the Japanese government to the 2000 tribunal has been a muted "apology and remorse", but no direct acceptance of liability or adoption of the various recommendations included in the tribunal's final judgment.

Symbolically, the conclusions from the Women's Tribunal of 2000 are an indictment of all governments and militaries that have permitted or actively encouraged sexual violence in war and failed to prosecute the perpetrators, let alone accept legal responsibility. The tribunal also pointed out to governments that the voices of victims of sexual violence cannot be silenced forever and that international civil society is increasing its demand for exposure and prosecution of these crimes.

Tradition of impunity

Violence against women in conflict situations assumes many forms; rape is often only one of the ways in which women are targeted. As Graça Machel noted in her report, Impact of Armed Conflict on Children, "While abuses such as murder and torture have long been denounced as war crimes, rape has been downplayed as an unfortunate but inevitable side effect of war."[1] It has therefore been largely ignored as a human

rights abuse. However, some observers identify a new, evolving attitude with respect to the prosecution of sexual violence committed during armed conflict as serious international crimes. The international community has, it seems, increased its efforts to end the cycle of impunity for these crimes.

The global failure to punish rapists whether in times of peace or conflict appears to be as consistent and widespread as the crime of rape itself. There has been little improvement in even acknowledging the gravity of rape as a wartime abuse, and such acts are largely unpunished. Some "big fish" commanders and perpetrators with political profiles have been prosecuted, but millions of women in the post-conflict Democratic Republic of Congo (DRC), Liberia, Sierra Leone or Colombia, for example, have faint hope of their abusers being brought to justice.

"How is it that rape, a crime universally condemned, can be disregarded and trivialized when it occurs in war?" asked two researchers in 1994, as hard data of the scale of systematic rape in the Balkan conflict emerged.[2] As most commentators observe, no new laws are required to prosecute such cases. The existing international legal framework of humanitarian law, human rights law and criminal law — although not always sufficiently explicit — clearly prohibits and criminalises sexual violence and sexual slavery and provides universal jurisdiction in most cases.[3] The problem lies not in the law, but in the failure to enforce it.

For many analysts and activists, the issue is the mischaracterisation of rape as a sexual crime against individual women and their honour, rather than as a violation of the victim's physical integrity and human rights. The failure to recognise that widespread rape is a mechanism to punish, humiliate and terrorise women and entire communities during conflict has contributed to the failure to denounce and prosecute wartime rape.

In addition to increased media and international attention to sexual violence during conflict since the early 1990s, the relevant legal framework has also developed considerably, in particular thanks to the establishment and subsequent jurisprudence from the ad hoc International Criminal Tribunal for the former Yugoslavia (ICTY) and the International Criminal Tribunal for Rwanda (ICTR), both established by the United Nations Security Council.

Initially, groups such as the US-based Human Rights Watch feared the precedential value of the ad hoc tribunals of the early 1990s was at risk

A US soldier takes cover inside the doorway of an Iraqi home. In the context of Iraq, the presence of foreign, non-Muslim forces is offensive to many communities. Their entry into private homes – the protected domain of women and girls in such conservative societies – is considered unacceptable. Insecurity at home is reportedly a source of increasing anxiety for women in Iraq, where sexual attacks are rising in proportion to the growing lawlessness.

Image: Brent Stirton

Agnes Piloya shows scars from the beatings she endured while being held captive by the Lord's Resistance Army (LRA) in northern Uganda. After her abduction on 5 August 1995, she was forced to become the "wife" of an LRA commander. She escaped once, but was quickly captured. Upon her recapture, she was tied to a tree to be executed, the price to pay for escaping. She survived, however, because a commander – who inquired if she had been re-captured and was told by a soldier that she was about to be shot – immediately sent the order not to kill her. She was then given to serve as the "wife" of another man, a sergeant with whom she had two children. Gulu, northern Uganda, November 2005.

Image: Guillaume Bonn

Girls who were recently liberated from the LRA at the Gusco Rehabilitation Centre in northern Uganda. Many of them were abducted and made to serve LRA combatants. Some were forced to fight and kill, and most were forced to act as "wives" of commanders, enduring months or years of rape. Many of the girls who released or escaped have borne their abductor's children. For most LRA victims, the struggle for economic survival and to come to peace with their past is a daily battle, and the notion of seeking justice or reparations is inconceivable.

Image: Sven Torfinn / OCHA

of being limited to rhetorical posturing by the UN. What was initially seen as foot-dragging by the UN and reluctance by the member states to fully fund the courts, however, did result in genuine convictions and sentencing, and their work continues to this day. The fear that amnesties would be traded in exchange for peace was assuaged by firm indictments, prosecution and unequivocal judgements in both *ad hoc* courts as well as in the Special Court of Sierra Leone.

A new breed of courts

Genocide, crimes against humanity and war crimes, all of which encompass sexual violence, are deemed to be the most heinous international offences. Crimes of this nature can be prosecuted by domestic courts, international courts such as the ICTY/R or the International Criminal Court (ICC), and the new breed of popular internationalised or hybrid courts.[4]

Both international and internationalised courts have been established with considerable UN involvement and share the same fundamental goal: to "sanction serious violations of international law (in particular, international humanitarian law, and human rights law) committed by individuals and, as a consequence, deter future violations and help to re-establish the rule of law"[5] in post-conflict societies. Like the *ad hoc* tribunals, internationalised courts — such as the Crimes Panels of the District Court of Dili (Timor-Leste); "Regulation 64" Panels in the courts of Kosovo; and the Special Court for Sierra Leone — are *ad hoc* in that they have been created for particular circumstances and for a limited timeframe. They are mandated to prosecute individuals and rely on international cooperation, funding and judicial assistance. However, internationalised courts differ from international courts in a number of important respects: They can be part of the judiciary of a particular country or "grafted" onto the local judicial system[6]; they are composed of both international and local staff; and they apply a mix of international and national law. International courts, in contrast, operate outside the jurisdiction in which the crimes were committed, apply international law and employ international staff.

The ICC – which was established on 1 July 2002 under the Rome Statute – is the first permanent international judicial body capable of trying individuals for genocide, crimes against humanity and war crimes. Its statute is a product of considerable lobbying by NGOs and civil-society groups in an effort to end impunity for international crimes, including those of a sexual nature. Amnesty International referred to the statute as the "first international treaty to expressly recognise a broad spectrum of sexual and gender-based violence as some of the gravest crimes under international law."[7]

According to the UN Special Rapporteur on Violence Against Women, "The Rome Statute's gender provisions are an encouraging example of how the development of the international women's rights movement is positively impacting international human rights and humanitarian law despite the strong influence of conservative political forces [...] While much remains to be done, the progress made since 1994 is extraordinary."[8]

The general concept behind the ICC is the notion that the prosecution of international crimes is primarily the task of individual states, under the principle of complementarity. According to Article 17 of the statute, the prosecution of crimes before the court "is only admissible if and to the extent that an effective prosecution at the national level is thwarted by legal or factual obstacles."[9] States that have ratified the statute, therefore, are obliged to introduce or amend their criminal laws to enable them to prosecute international crimes themselves. If a state is unable or unwilling to prosecute the crimes within its domestic courts, a case may be referred to the ICC by the UN Security Council or the ICC

> "...the "first international treaty to expressly recognise a broad spectrum of sexual and gender-based violence as some of the gravest crimes under international law."

prosecutor or initiated by another state party to the treaty. A state may be determined to be "unwilling" to prosecute if it is clearly shielding someone from responsibility for ICC crimes, while "unable" means the domestic legal system has collapsed.[10]

Obligations to prosecute international crimes at a national level also flow from other international treaties, such as the Geneva Conventions (for grave breaches of international humanitarian law), the Convention on the Prevention and Punishment of the Crime of Genocide, and the Convention Against Torture and Other Cruel, Degrading or Inhuman Treatment or Punishment, which are legally binding.

In addition, the perception of a duty to prosecute cases of genocide, grave breaches of international humanitarian law and torture, all of which are considered crimes under international customary law,[11] is reportedly gaining ground.

National responsibilities and limitations

Grave breaches of the Geneva Conventions attract universal jurisdiction and therefore can be prosecuted by an international tribunal or by the domestic courts of any country. This mechanism for holding war criminals accountable, however, is available only for crimes committed in international conflicts.

In 1973, the UN adopted a resolution in which it noted in particular that "[e]very State has the right to try its own nationals for war crimes or crimes against humanity."[12] This principle also applies to cases of sexual violence.

Wherever national courts have established adequate procedural mechanisms to safeguard the rights of both victims and defendants, national prosecutions for violations of human rights and humanitarian law may often be preferable to prosecutions before international tribunals. Local populations (often including victims) need to see justice performed in their own country; the process enhances the legitimacy of

Even if there is international political will to prosecute cases of sexual violence, current humanitarian law provides little authority to the international community to oblige or force a state to account for its conduct during an internal conflict.

the national judiciary if performed well. In addition, the whole process can be faster and far less expensive. However, the prosecution of violent sexual crimes requires specific procedural and evidentiary safeguards to ensure that national prosecutions adequately respond to the violations.[13] In many cases the forensic evidence is not available, or cannot be relied upon, and also witness protection cannot be guaranteed.

Even if there is international political will to prosecute cases of sexual violence, current humanitarian law provides little authority to the international community to oblige or force a state to account for its conduct during an internal conflict.

Many countries fail their responsibilities because the domestic laws that would be used to prosecute wartime rape classify the crime in ways that minimise its seriousness and allow the possibility of discriminatory prosecution. In Liberia and the DRC, vicious internal conflicts have raged and thousands of cases of rape and sexual violence – often of an extreme nature in terms of brutality – have been reported. Yet in both countries there have been almost no successful prosecutions and convictions for wartime (or peacetime) rape. These examples are as

much a testimony to the inefficiency of local legal systems as they are to the dominant traditional male values that trivialise the crime of rape.

A key concern in evaluating the competence of national judicial systems to try international crimes is the extent to which the national legal system protects the rights of women. A legal system's general approach towards crimes of sexual violence may be an additional important factor to consider when evaluating the overall utility of national rather than international prosecutions for acts of rape and sexual slavery committed during armed conflict. In national prosecutions, such cases should generally be tried as international rather than municipal crimes, with the application, therefore, of international procedural rules on issues such as the admissibility of evidence.

A general survey of municipal legal systems in a wide selection of countries revealed the following examples of gender-based discrimination codified in criminal laws and justice systems: rape and other forms of sexual assault being defined as crimes against the community rather than against the individual victim, even though nonsexual assaults are defined as crimes against the individual victim; rape being defined as an act committed by a man against a woman (not his wife), even though men are also victims of sexual violence; procedural laws requiring women to take independent action to initiate the prosecution of rape cases by the prosecutor's office; evidentiary laws that accord less weight to evidence that is presented by a woman; evidentiary laws in rape and sexual assault cases requiring women to provide corroborating testimony from men; substantive laws allowing a married woman who is unsuccessful in proving that she has been raped to then be charged with adultery; provisions allowing a man convicted of rape to avoid punishment if he marries the victim; laws preventing women from serving as judges or fact-finders; laws restricting women's access to abortions, contraception or reproductive information; and the absence of adequate, gender-specific witness-protection programmes – leaving survivors of sexual and gender-based violence vulnerable to retaliatory attacks and at the mercy of their male relatives, who often regard the survivors as "dishonoured women".[14] Some legal systems emphasise the immoral status of rape survivors rather than the violent nature of the offence committed by the perpetrator.

More specifically, Peru's laws once designated rape a crime against honour; currently rape is defined as a crime against *libertad sexual* (the

Bosnian Serb rapist Dragoljub Kunarac shocked the United Nations International War Crimes Tribunal for the former Yugoslavia (ICTY) in his initial court appearance by pleading guilty in 1998 to raping Muslim women. During the Balkans conflict, there was widespread and systematic use of rape by all belligerents — in particular the Serbian forces. During the ICTY trials, rape, which was closely associated with ethnic cleansing, was officially recognised for the first time as a war crime.

Image: Jerry Lampen/AFP

Soldiers of the new Iraqi army enter a suspicious building. With the proliferation of armed groups, paramilitary units, insurgents and criminals, murders and executions take place on a daily basis. Human Rights Watch released a report in July 2003, entitled Climate of Fear: Sexual Violence and Abduction of Women and Girls in Baghdad, which found that "police officers gave low priority to allegations of sexual violence and abduction, that the police were under-resourced, and that victims of sexual violence confronted indifference and sexism from Iraqi law enforcement personnel." Since then, as chaos, violence and bloodletting have descended on Iraq, matters for women and girls have reportedly become worse.

Image: Brent Stirton

freedom to choose a sexual partner) and not as a physical assault. In many countries and some parts of the US, there is no legal concept of marital rape. Turkey's criminal code classifies rape as a "felony against public decency and family order" and not — as are other types of assault and battery — as a "felony against an individual". In Pakistan, evidentiary laws discriminate against women by granting no legal weight to their testimony in certain rape trials.[15] In these contexts, where rape is inaccurately – and insultingly — defined, the likelihood that perpetrators will be brought to justice is slim. Women often find that their honour, instead of the rapist's crime, is on trial.

Whenever possible, concluded the UN's special rapporteur, cases involving claims of sexual slavery or sexual violence should be tried in domestic courts as international crimes rather than municipal crimes, with alternative charges under municipal law in case the necessary elements of the international crime cannot be established.[16]

In addition, local prosecutions may be more effective in preventing future violations, while facilitating the return of victims to their pre-war communities, by removing some of the stigma that may often be attached, however improperly, to victims of sexual violence. However, because of culturally maintained gender stereotypes, it is not self-evident that all survivors of such violations will be willing or able to come forward, either because they fear exposing themselves to further stigma or because they fear retaliation. Thus, local tribunals in post-conflict proceedings must be evaluated based on their ability to ensure the rights of both victims and defendants to obtain justice before an independent and impartial tribunal.[17]

Important judicial precedents ICTY and ICTR

Different types of sexual violence may constitute different crimes. Acts such as rape, sexual assault, sexual slavery, forced prostitution and forced pregnancy may be charged under both domestic and international law.[18] It is possible to charge an individual with a crime such as rape under domestic law as well as under international law as a crime against humanity or war crime.[19] Both charges may focus on the same events, but each crime contains different elements that must be proven, as well as different evidential standards.

During the 1990s, the ICTY/R made significant strides in protecting women's rights by interpreting sexual violence as an abuse of both international humanitarian law and human rights law and bringing

perpetrators to justice, as well as setting important precedents for the ICC and hybrid and national courts.[20]

More than 20,000 Bosnian women are thought to have been raped during the war. Most analysts consider that there is little doubt this figure is an underestimate due to underreporting. In September 1992, a number of reports emerged citing systematic rape of women and girls in Bosnia and Herzegovina. A subsequent report by the Bosnia and Herzegovina government cited evidence of the rape by Serbs of at least 13,000 women and girls, the majority of whom were Muslim. In the conservative Muslim communities of Bosnia, rape brought considerable shame upon the victim and severely affected her future status in her community, so it is expected that these figures are considerably lower than reality. A follow-up study

> Some women were specifically kept in 'rape camps' until they were not only pregnant but beyond the date that abortions can be safely performed.

by the European Commission suggested that the numbers were around 20,000, which is currently the figure most quoted.

An estimated 1 percent to 4 percent of raped women became pregnant during the wars in the former Yugoslavia. Some women were specifically kept in "rape camps" until they were not only pregnant but beyond the date that abortions could be safely performed.

In Rwanda, according to a 1996 Human Rights Watch Report on Sexual Violence, an estimated 250,000 women were raped during the 100-day genocide in 1994. The so-called "children of hate" or "pregnancies of war" are numbered by the Rwanda National Population Office at 2,000 to 5,000. In one interesting case at the ICTR, Pauline Nyiramasuhuko became the first woman charged with genocide and using rape as a crime against humanity.

The tribunals have successfully prosecuted acts of sexual violence as war crimes, crimes against humanity and as instruments of genocide and have clarified the relationship between rape, persecution and torture.[21] They have also found those who encourage, order, assist or facilitate sexual violence to be liable.

International crimes

Rape contravenes international law at different levels. Sexual violation rises to the level of a war crime or a grave breach of the Geneva

Conventions regardless of whether it occurs on a demonstrably massive scale or is associated with an overarching policy. Individual rapes that function as torture or cruel and inhuman treatment themselves constitute grave breaches of the Geneva Conventions. Thus, even if rape occurs in an apparently indiscriminate fashion and not in the service of a large-scale, overarching strategic policy, it is a violation of international law. When rape occurs on a massive scale or as a matter of orchestrated policy, this added dimension of the crime is recognised by designating and prosecuting rape as a crime against humanity.[22]

On the international level, rape has been afforded a new legal status by certain groundbreaking statutes and convictions that have seen the crime included in prosecution of genocide, crimes against humanity and war crimes.

1. Genocide

The 1998 conviction by the ICTR of former Rwandan mayor Jean Paul Akayesu on nine counts of genocide and crimes against humanity (including rape, torture and other inhumane acts) and for his role in

In its analysis of the various elements of the crime of genocide, the ICTR found in Akayesu that sexual violence could be committed with the intention of destroying a group.

encouraging and inciting rape was a landmark judgment. It was the first-ever genocide conviction under international law, and in addition the trial chamber reached the conclusion that sexual violence constituted the crime of genocide. Commenting on the conviction, the then-chief prosecutor for the ICTR and ICTY, Louise Arbour, said the judgment was "a major concrete step" in the destruction of the culture of impunity.[23] "The judgment is truly remarkable in its breadth and vision, as well as in the detailed legal analysis on many issues that will be critical to the future of both ICTR and ICTY, in particular with respect to the law of sexual violence," she said[24].

Genocide includes any of the following acts committed with intent to destroy in whole or in part, a national, ethnic, racial or religious group:
    a) killing members of the group;
    b) causing serious bodily or mental harm to members of the group;
    c) deliberately inflicting on the group conditions of life calculated to bring about its physical destruction in whole or in part;
    d) imposing measures intended to prevent births within the group;
    e) forcibly transferring children of the group to another group.[25]

In its analysis of the various elements of the crime of genocide, the ICTR found in Akayesu that sexual violence could be committed with the intention of destroying a group. "These rapes resulted in physical and psychological destruction of Tutsi women, their families and their communities. Sexual violence was an integral part of the process of destruction, specifically targeting Tutsi women and specifically contributing to their destruction and to the destruction of the Tutsi group as a whole," the trial chamber held.[26]

2. Crimes against humanity

Rape and torture were for the first time explicitly included as crimes against humanity in the statute of the ICTY in 1993, followed by the ICTR a year later.

Crimes against humanity, according to the statutes of both the ICTY and the ICTR, include murder; extermination; enslavement; deportation; imprisonment; torture; rape; persecutions on political, racial and religious grounds; and other inhumane acts. In the case of former Yugoslavia, these crimes were crimes against humanity when committed during armed conflict, whether international or internal in character, and directed against any civilian population. For Rwanda, they were considered crimes against humanity when committed "as part of a widespread or systematic attack against any civilian population on national, political, ethnic, racial or religious grounds."

3. Violations of the laws of war

The ICTR and ICTY have been successful in their prosecutions of rape as a war-crime. By prosecuting rapists under war-crimes legislation, the courts have attacked the widely held notion that rape is a regrettable yet inevitable by-product of conflict and proven that rape is deliberately and systematically used as part of military strategies.

Two child amputees in Sierra Leone. The Revolutionary United Front (RUF) rebels' cruel tactics of terror resulted in an estimated 100,000 amputations. Not only was rape widely practiced by the RUF and other armed groups in Sierra Leone and Liberia, but women and young children, even babies, were deliberately mutilated. Having lost their men in the bloodshed, women – already more vulnerable to sexual attack during conflict – have been forced to bear the additional burden of caring for the wounded and malnourished as well as rebuilding the lives of their families.

Image: Brent Stirton

Bukavu, Democratic Republic of Congo, 2005. "This image shows a man and woman who appeared out of the forest and stopped a UN patrol of Pakistani peacekeepers. The woman is carrying her dead husband on her back; the man with her is her brother-in-law. Her husband and brother-in-law had been kidnapped by a militia group and held to ransom. Despite a bullet wound and severe injuries from torture and being bound by barbed wire, the two men managed to escape. The women's husband died shortly after reaching home from the trauma of his experience, and the brother-in-law remained catatonic the entire time I saw them. Shortly after the UN troops recorded their details for investigation, the woman walked slowly back into the forest with her dead husband on her back and her silent brother-in-law alongside her. Such is the resignation to terror in the civilian population it has become the norm." (Excerpt from the photographer's notes.) A culture of impunity pervades many conflict situations, where men as well as women are subject to random violence and abuse. They can expect neither justice nor restitution, nor even recognition.

Image: Brent Stirton

Treaty law and customary international humanitarian law are the main sources, or origins of recognised humanitarian law,[27] which consists of "a whole system of legal safeguards that cover the way wars may be fought and the protection of individuals"[28] and is essentially contained within the following texts:

- The various declarations and conventions of The Hague (1899, 1907, 1954, 1957, 1970 and 1973), which lay down the rules for the conduct of hostilities.[29]
- The four Geneva Conventions of 1949, which codify the rules and customs of the laws of war, adding rules governing assistance to and protection of non-combatants[30], specifically the wounded (first Geneva Convention), wounded and shipwrecked at sea (second convention), prisoners of war (third convention) and civilians under enemy control (fourth convention).
- The two additional protocols to the Geneva Conventions adopted in 1977 to improve protection for victims of war during international armed conflict (first protocol) and non-international armed conflict (second protocol). The second protocol "takes account of anti-colonial wars and the civil wars which succeeded them"[31] and is an addition to the protection afforded by Article 3 of each of the four 1949 Geneva Conventions, which governs wars that are non-international.[32]

In the Hague Conventions, there is only one article (Art 46, 4th Hague Agreement of 1907) that implicitly forbids sexual violence, stating, "Family honour and rights, the lives of persons, and private property, as well as religious convictions and practice, must be respected."

The four Geneva Conventions of 1949, drawn up in the aftermath of World War II, consist of 429 articles, yet only one (Art 27, para 2, 4th Geneva Convention) explicitly forbids rape and forced prostitution.[33] The 1977 protocols include just three explicit prohibitions of rape and forced prostitution.[34] No mention is made of sexual violence in the "grave breach" provisions, contained within each of the four conventions, which states are obliged to make subject to the jurisdiction of domestic courts, although current interpretation of these provisions allows for rape prosecutions.[35]

Thus, it has been argued by many feminist writers and advocates of women's rights that international humanitarian law "takes a particular male perspective on armed conflict."[36] Helen Durham writes, "In a world where women are not equals of men, and armed conflict impacts upon men and women in a fundamentally different way, a general category of rules that is not inclusive of the reality for women cannot respond to their situation."[37]

Some analysts have also complained that provisions in international humanitarian law are often articulated in terms of protection, rather than a blanket prohibition of sexual violence or the guarantee of the right of women and girls not to be subject to sexual violence.[38]

Both statutes of the ICTY and ICTR extended jurisdiction over grave breaches of the Geneva Conventions and other war crimes. The ICTY statute includes "torture or inhumane treatment" and "willfully causing great suffering or serious injury to body or health" within this category. The ICTR statute went a step further, specifically including humiliating and degrading treatment, rape, enforced prostitution and any form of indecent assault as war crimes.

The first judgment of the ICTY concerning sexual violence as a war crime was made in 1998.[39] The court recognised the rapes of Bosnian Serb women at the Celibici Prison Camp as acts of torture, finding Hazim Delic, a deputy camp commander, guilty of torture as both a grave breach of the Geneva Conventions and a war crime.[40] The camp commander, Zdravko Mucic, was also found to have command responsibility for crimes committed at the camp, including sexual assault.[41]

In the separate trial, military commander Anto Furundzija[42] was found guilty as a co-perpetrator of torture and of aiding and abetting outrages upon personal dignity, including rape committed by a third party. Notably, unlike crimes against humanity, a war crime can be a single and isolated act.

First definition of rape in international law

The Akayesu judgment by the ICTR was the first to explicitly examine the crime of rape as a crime against humanity and included the first definition of rape in international law. "The Chamber defines rape as a physical invasion of a sexual nature, committed on a person under

"In a world where women are not equals of men, and armed conflict impacts upon men and women in a fundamentally different way, a general category of rules that is not inclusive of the reality for women cannot respond to their situation."

circumstances which are coercive. Sexual violence which includes rape is considered to be any act of a sexual nature which is committed on a person under circumstances which are coercive." Moreover, the judgment stated, "Sexual violence is not limited to physical invasion of the human body and may include acts which do not involve penetration or even physical contact.

"Coercive circumstances need not be evidenced by a show of physical force. Threats, intimidation, extortion and other forms of duress which prey on fear or desperation may constitute coercion, and coercion may be inherent in certain circumstances ..."[43]

However, a different definition of rape has since been used by other *ad hoc* tribunals. In Kunarac, Kovac and Vokovic, the ICTY trial chamber adopted a narrower definition that specified penetration, which was

> In addition to sexual enslavement, sexual violence can also constitute torture, persecution and "other inhumane acts", as per the above definitions of crimes against humanity.

later confirmed by the appeals chamber. It held that in international law, rape was constituted by "the sexual penetration, however slight: (a) of the vagina or anus of the victim by the penis of the perpetrator or any other object used by the perpetrator; or (b) of the mouth of the victim by the penis of the perpetrator; where such sexual penetration occurs without the consent of the victim ... Consent for this purpose must be consent given voluntarily, as a result of the victim's free will, assessed in the context of the surrounding circumstances. The *mens rea*[44] is the intention to effect this sexual penetration, and the knowledge that it occurs without the consent of the victim."[45]

Two years later, the ICTR trial chamber adopted a narrower definition in Semanza, stating that "while this mechanical style of defining rape was originally rejected by this Tribunal, the Chamber finds the comparative analysis in Kunarac to be persuasive and thus will adopt the definition of rape approved by the ICTY Appeals Chamber. The Chamber recognises that other acts of sexual violence that do not satisfy this narrow definition may be prosecuted as other crimes against humanity [...] such as torture, persecution, enslavement, or other inhumane acts."[46]

Kunarac, Kovac and Vokovic was the second major international trial dealing with crimes of a sexual nature and led to three Bosnian Serb men being found guilty of multiple rape, torture and sexual enslavement of Muslim women. Rape had been successfully prosecuted at the ICTY

before[47], but this was the first case to deal exclusively with rape and enslavement and the first to rule that rape and enslavement were crimes against humanity. Significantly, although two of the survivors had been sold by Radomir Kovac, the court found that enslavement did not necessarily require the buying or selling of a human being.[48]

In addition to sexual enslavement, sexual violence can also constitute torture, persecution and "other inhumane acts", as per the above definitions of crime s against humanity.

Other courts have also sought to expand the jurisprudence on crimes against humanity. The prosecution at the hybrid Special Court for Sierra Leone has pushed the borders of international law by including the charge of "forced marriage" as a crime against humanity in its indictments against the Revolutionary United Front and Armed Forces Revolutionary Council.[49] This serves to criminalise the forced imposition of the status of marriage, with its resultant expectations of sexual access and the undertaking of domestic duties. Notably, sexual slavery, which is often a consequence of forced marriage, continues to be charged as a separate crime against humanity.

Sexual violence is addressed in different legal instruments and has been identified in different ways through different court interpretations and findings. Here are some examples from ITCR illustrating the power of existing legislation to condemn rape and sexual violence in war:

Sexual violence qualifying as serious bodily or mental harm: "Serious bodily or mental harm [...] include[s] acts of bodily or mental torture, inhumane or degrading treatment, rape, sexual violence, and persecution." Rutaganda, trial chamber, 6 December 1999, para [51].

Sexual violence qualifying as a condition of life calculated to bring about the physical destruction of a group in whole or in part: "The conditions of life envisaged include rape [...]" Kayishema and Ruzindana, trial chamber, 21 May 1999, para 548.

Sexual violence imposing measures intended to prevent births within the group: Includes "sexual mutilation, the practice of sterilisation, forced birth control, separation of the sexes and prohibition of marriages. In patriarchal societies, where membership of a group is determined by the identity of the father, an example [...] is the case where, during rape, a woman of the said group is deliberately impregnated by a man of

A young Iraqi woman puts on the veil for the first time as she comes of age and prepares to leave her home. However, the streets are dangerous. "After the American invasion, local gangs began roaming Baghdad, snatching girls and women from the street. [...] No one knows how many abducted women have never returned. As one Iraqi police inspector testified, 'Some gangs specialize in kidnapping girls, they sell them to Gulf countries. This happened before the war too, but now it is worse, they can get in and out without passports.' Others interviewed by Human Rights Watch argued that such trafficking in women had not occurred before the invasion. The US State Department's June 2005 report on the trafficking of women suggested that the extent of the problem in Iraq is 'difficult to appropriately gauge' under current chaotic circumstances, but cited an unknown number of Iraqi women and girls being sent to Yemen, Syria, Jordan, and Persian Gulf countries for sexual exploitation." (Excerpt from The Hidden War on Women in Iraq, by Ruth Rosen, July 2006.)

Image: Brent Stirton

another group, with the intent to have her give birth to a child who will consequently not belong to its mother's group." Akayesu, trial chamber, 2 September 1998, para 507-508.

Requirement of involvement of a public official for rape to constitute torture

"Like torture, rape is a violation of personal dignity, and rape in fact constitutes torture when inflicted by or at the instigation of or with the consent or acquiescence of a public official or other person acting in an official capacity."[50]

"In Akayesu, the Trial Chamber relied on the definition of torture found in the [...] Convention Against Torture [...] The ICTY Appeals Chamber has since explained that while the definition contained in the Convention Against Torture is reflective of customary international law [...], it is not identical to the definition of torture as a crime against humanity. The ICTY Appeals Chamber has confirmed that, outside the framework of the Convention Against Torture, the 'public official' requirement is not a requirement under customary international law in relation to individual criminal responsibility for torture as a crime against humanity."[51]

Rape constituting persecution

"The ICTY has found that the following acts may constitute persecution when committed with the requisite discriminatory intent: imprisonment, unlawful detention of civilians or infringement upon individual freedom, murder, deportation or forcible transfer, seizure, collection, segregation and forced transfer of civilians to camps, comprehensive destruction of homes and property, the destruction of towns, villages and other public or private property and the plunder of property, attacks upon cities, towns and villages, trench-digging and the use of hostages and human shields, the destruction and damage of religious or educational institutions, and sexual violence."[52]

A single act may constitute persecution if discriminatory intent is proven

"Persecution was often used to describe a series of acts. However, the Trial Chamber does not exclude the possibility that a single act may constitute persecution. In such a case, there must be clear evidence of the discriminatory intent."[53]

Rape falling within the scope of "other inhumane acts"

Akayesu was "judged criminally responsible [...] for the following other inhumane acts: (i) the forced undressing of [a woman] outside the bureau communal, after making her sit in the mud [...]; (ii) the forced undressing and public marching of [a woman] naked at the bureau communal; (iii) the forced undressing of [three women] and the forcing of the women to perform exercises naked in public near the bureau communal."[54]

Sexual violence as torture: a violation of international humanitarian law

The criteria for rape as torture were defined in detail by the ICTY trial chamber in 1998: The criteria for "the elements of torture, for the purposes of applying Articles 2 and 3 of the Statute, may be enumerated as follows: (i) There must be an act or omission that causes severe pain or suffering, whether mental or physical, (ii) which is inflicted intentionally, (iii) and for such purposes as obtaining information or a confession from the victim, or a third person, punishing the victim for an act he or she or a third person has committed or is suspected of having committed, intimidating or coercing the victim or a third person, or for any reason based on discrimination of any kind, (iv) and such act or omission being committed by, or at the instigation of, or with the consent or acquiescence of, an official or other person acting in an official capacity."[55]

More details of this definition are included in the findings of the ICTY appeals chamber. "The first element for the crime of torture is "the infliction, by act or omission, of severe pain or suffering, whether physical or mental [...] Some acts establish *per se* the suffering of those upon whom they were inflicted. Rape is [...] such an act. [...] Sexual violence necessarily gives rise to severe pain or suffering, whether physical or mental, and in this way justifies its characterisation as an act of torture. Severe pain or suffering, as required by the definition of the crime of torture, can thus be said to be established once rape has been proved, since the act of rape necessarily implies such pain or suffering."[56]

Recognition of rape in the Rome Statute of the ICC

Article 7(1)of the ICC statute recognises that rape, sexual slavery, trafficking, enforced prostitution, forced pregnancy,[57] enforced sterilisation, or any other form of sexual violence of comparable gravity, when conducted "as part of a widespread or systematic attack directed against any civilian population, with knowledge of the attack" can amount to crimes against humanity. This was the very first time the crimes of sexual slavery and trafficking had been expressly recognised as crimes against humanity in an international treaty.[58]

The Rome Statute also provides that acts of rape, sexual slavery, enforced prostitution, forced pregnancy, enforced sterilisation and any other form of sexual violence constitute a grave breach or serious violation of common Article 3 of the Geneva Conventions may be prosecuted as war crimes.[59] This is the case whether they occur during international or non-international – civil or internal – armed conflict.

Rape and other forms of sexual violence have been defined broadly in the ICC elements of crimes to focus on the coercive acts of the perpetrator, including threats and psychological force.[60] Instead of defining rape in terms of forced penetration with a penis, the definition is gender-neutral, acknowledging that men and boys may also be raped, and refers generally to the invasion of the victim's body, which could include rape with objects and forced oral sex.[61]

" ...Severe pain or suffering, as required by the definition of the crime of torture, can thus be said to be established once rape has been proved, since the act of rape necessarily implies such pain or suffering."

Human rights law

Human rights law contains provisions governing sexual violence, but enforcement mechanisms are weak or non-existent in many countries. The UN Convention on the Elimination of all Forms of Discrimination Against Women (adopted by the General Assembly in 1979) contains no mention of sexual violence, but notably the quasi-judicial committee that monitors adherence to the treaty has defined gender-based violence committed against a woman because she is a woman, as including "acts that inflict physical, mental or sexual harm or suffering, threats of such acts, coercion and other deprivations of liberty."[62]

The 1993 Declaration on the Elimination of Violence Against Women and the Global Platform for Action,[63] adopted in Beijing in 1995, reiterate the responsibility of states to protect women from sexual violence. The more recent Brussels Call to Action to Address Sexual Violence in Conflict called for urgent and long-term action to "intensify international, regional and national efforts to end impunity for perpetrators by strengthening the legal and judicial systems and by enacting and enforcing legislation, and provide national justice systems with the necessary resources to prosecute cases of sexual and gender-based violence."[64] However, while these commitments are politically binding, they are not legally binding.

UN Security Council Resolution 1325 sends a strong message to all governments, UN bodies and parties to armed conflict that special efforts must be made to protect the human rights of women and girls in conflict situations. It calls on "all parties to armed conflict to take special

measures to protect women and girls from gender-based violence, particularly rape and other forms of sexual abuse, and all other forms of violence in situations of armed conflict" and "emphasises the responsibility of all States to put an end to impunity and to prosecute those responsible for genocide, crimes against humanity, war crimes including those relating to sexual violence against women and girls, and in this regard, stresses the need to exclude these crimes, where feasible, from amnesty provisions."[65]

Recent regional human rights instruments, which are technically legally binding (although difficult and in many cases impossible to enforce), provide more explicit protection. The Inter-American Convention on the Prevention, Punishment and Eradication of Violence Against Women, adopted in 1994, obliges states to protect women from physical, sexual and psychological violence within the family/domestic unit, community or at the hands of or condoned by the state or its agents, including rape, battery and sexual abuse, torture, trafficking in persons, forced prostitution, kidnapping and sexual harassment.[66]

The Protocol to the African Charter on Human and Peoples' Rights on the Rights of Women in Africa, adopted in 2003, contains a provision on the protection of women in armed conflict, obliging states to "protect asylum seeking women, refugees, returnees and internally displaced persons, against all forms of violence, rape and other forms of sexual exploitation, and to ensure that such acts are considered war crimes, genocide and/or crimes against humanity and that their perpetrators are brought to justice before a competent criminal jurisdiction."[67]

Furthermore, African states are obliged to uphold women's right to health, including sexual and reproductive health, which includes women's right to control their fertility, the right to decide whether to have children and the number of children and the spacing of children, the right to choose a method of contraception and the right to be protected against sexually transmitted infections, including HIV/AIDS.

Rape as part of a larger prejudice

Whether committed by an official of the state, militiaman or armed insurgent, whether as a result of specific policy or an individual incident

"It is the lack of political will that poses the greatest obstacle to the effective prosecution and redress of sexual slavery and sexual violence during armed conflict."

of torture or sexual opportunism, wartime rape constitutes an abuse of power and a violation of international humanitarian law. The fact that the impact and immediate effect of rape is similar to that of torture or cruel and inhuman treatment makes it even more alarming that it has not been prosecuted as such. "The differential treatment of rape underscores the fact that the problem—for the most part—lies not in the absence of adequate legal prohibitions, but in the international community's willingness to tolerate the subordination of women." [68]

Armed conflict exacerbates the discrimination and violence directed at women everywhere, every day. To end the cycle of violence, the equal right of women to participate in the economic, social, political and cultural life of their societies must be protected and promoted. "Without the full equality and participation of women, any steps taken to prevent systematic rape or sexual slavery during armed conflict or to rebuild societies recovering from war will ultimately fail."[69]

Political will to implement laws

The ICTR and the ICTY have "contributed groundbreaking international jurisprudence"[70] on sexual violence, but both have also been heavily criticised for not doing enough: "Barring dramatic

advances before the expiration of their respective mandates in 2010, in terms of sexual violence prosecutions each criminal tribunal risks being remembered for what it missed doing, rather than for what it achieved," according to Human Rights Watch. [71]

Human rights activists have observed that the tribunals' initial enthusiasm with regard to prosecuting crimes of a sexual nature has waned. Human Rights Watch has criticised both tribunals for failing to adopt effective long-term prosecution strategies that acknowledge the degree of wartime sexual violence that is suffered and accused them of failing to prioritise the issue after early landmark decisions.[72]

Activists insist that impunity for wartime rape must end and the international community must re-double its commitments in this regard. National governments, too, must hold those who commit rape in internal conflicts accountable and, where necessary, reform their laws to reflect the serious and substantive nature of the abuse.

International law must better reflect the experience of women and the true nature of the harm done to them, particularly during armed conflict, and the further development of the legal framework through consistent, gender-responsive practice is a critical goal. Nevertheless, according to the former UN Special Rapporteur on sexual violence, "It is the lack of political will that poses the greatest obstacle to the effective prosecution and redress of sexual slavery and sexual violence during armed conflict." ■

"The culture of the gun is deeply embedded in Afghanistan. Women and girls are at risk of abduction, sexual violence and intimidation as lawlessness spirals. Despite the ending of 23 years of conflict, a glut of weaponry remains in the hands of civilians, including ex-combatants. ' The first thing they do is rape the girl to stop her family seeking justice. […] When a girl loses her virginity she has no value. Usually, when families find that their girls have been raped by gunmen, they themselves ask them to marry their daughters. […] The Nijrab district is under the control of gunmen who kill people and rape and abduct the girls. No one stops them.' Seventeen-year-old Zarmina was abducted by three armed men from her aunt's home in Kapisa Province in Afghanistan in May 2004. Her uncle was shot and wounded as he tried to stop the men. Rape, forced marriage and the trafficking of women and children are rife.

The transitional government in Afghanistan has failed to provide security or to impose its rule throughout the country. Private armies and armed groups pose a constant threat. Powerful warlords and officials with a record of human rights violations flaunt their impunity with further abuses. Armed factions wield authority over provincial leaders and their security forces. The survivors of sexual violence often do not speak out. They face the very real danger of being killed by relatives for being seen as dishonouring the family or for 'immoral behaviour'. Most never receive justice for the crimes against them. Informal justice systems discriminate against women." (Excerpt from Stop Violence Against Women in Afghanistan – Abduction and Rape at the Point of a Gun, Amnesty International, 2004.)

Image: Thomas Grabka

Kibakuli's story

Kibakuli is 70 years old and comes from the village of Kanya Batundu, about 30km from Kitshanga in northeastern Democratic Republic of Congo. She was attacked by five militia. On the day of this interview, Kibakuli was given a goat, a hoe and some beans by Doctors On Call Services (DOCS), a nongovernmental agency that offers medical treatment, counselling and material support.

"I am from Kanya Batundu. I have three children and also look after four orphans. I came to Kitshanga after the attack. It was midnight when the attackers came. I was asleep, and my husband was visiting his sister in the village, so I was alone. There were five men. They came in and removed all my clothes. They stabbed me in the head and on the top of my arms with a machete, as they forced by hands back behind my head. I was screaming all the time as they raped me — all five of them, one by one. As one was raping me another would say: Get out so I can enter! They took me by force, causing my leg to hit against something. They beat my hand with a stick, and it is now damaged. My husband heard my screaming and came to find me. He was beaten with a gun; they beat him in the knees. I was in terrible pain. When they left I crawled out of the house. They were burning another house in the village and then they burned mine. They left me with fistula [a rupture of vaginal, bladder or rectal tissue reparable only through surgery], but I was cured by DOCS. I couldn't stay long with fistula, the smell was so bad from the urine. I went to DOCS and returned home in August 2004.

I am very, very happy today to receive the goat, beans and hoe. I have nothing. Look at the house [a mud hut with tiny, dusty room for cooking and a piece of cloth separating the sleeping area from the kitchen]. When the goat gives birth, I will give the first baby to DOCS. Because of the famine it will not be possible to sell the beans at the first harvest, but in the future I plan to sell them. I want to give part of my first harvest to DOCS; the rest I will use to feed my family. I am strong to cultivate."

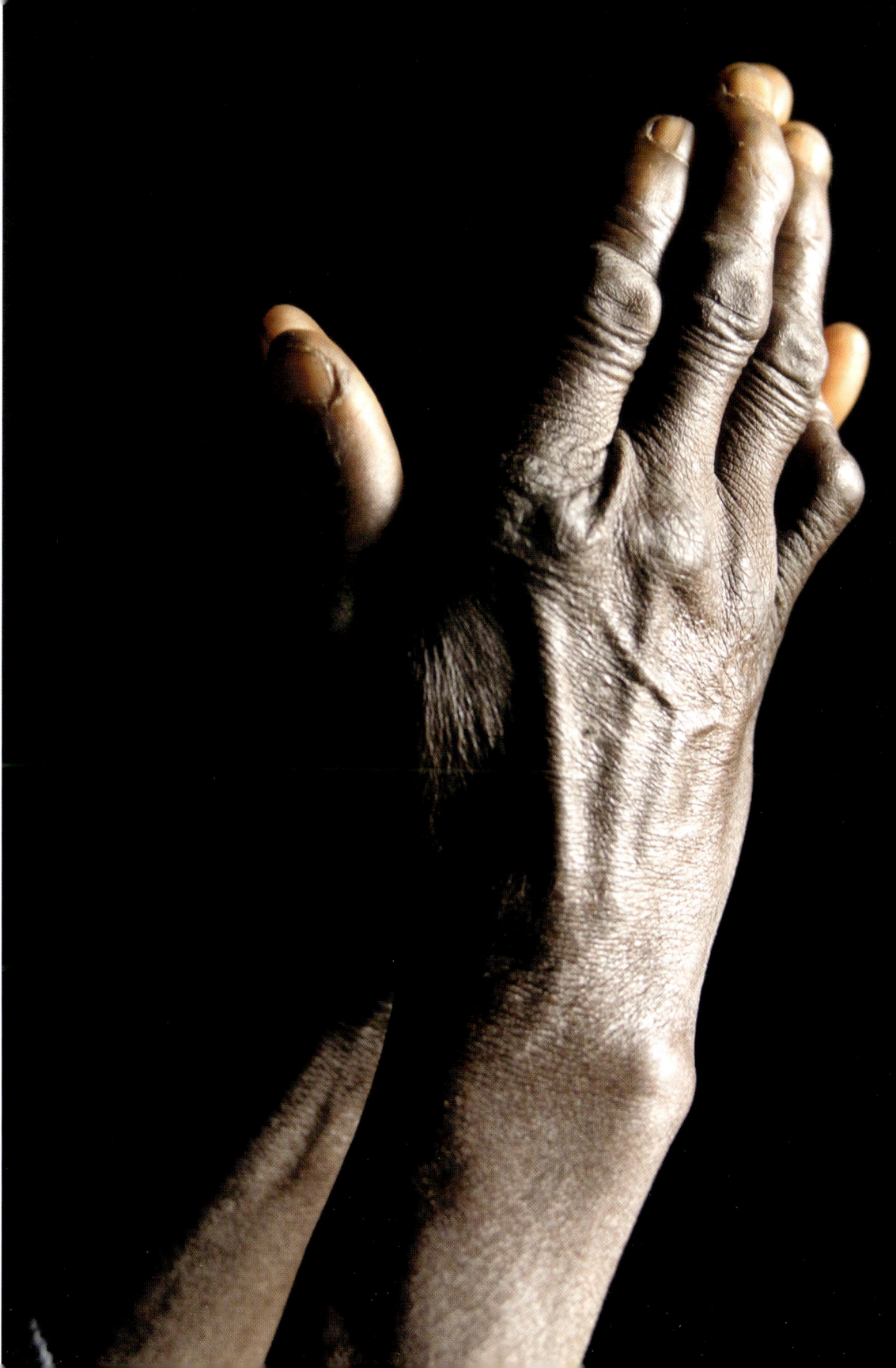

Image: Georgina Cranston

Allegations of sexual abuse and exploitation by United Nations peacekeepers in the Democratic Republic of the Congo, Liberia, Haiti and elsewhere have tarnished the reputation of the organisation. Speakers at a December 2006 meeting at UN headquarters in New York outlined a "zero-tolerance" policy and discussed innovative ways to fight sexual exploitation, including DNA sampling and an "anti-prostitution campaign" for 2007.

sexual abuse and exploitation by peacekeepers and aid workers

"Agency workers from the international and local NGOs as well as UN agencies were ranked as among the worst sex exploiters of children, often using the very humanitarian aid and services intended to benefit the refugee population as a tool of exploitation," concluded a 2001 United Nations High Commissioner for Refugees and Save the Children-UK investigation into allegations of sexual abuse and exploitation of refugees in Guinea, Liberia and Sierra Leone. Subsequent investigations by the UN's Office of Internal Oversight Services reached the same conclusion: Women and children were being raped and sexually abused by UN civilian and military personnel. (Sunday Standard report; Peacekeepers as predators: UN sex crimes by Tanonoka Joseph Whande, 29 January 2007)

UN Peacekeepers:
"One of the greatest stains on UN history" [1]

For more than a decade, informal reports have circulated about the behaviour of soldiers when abroad on peacekeeping assignments. In spite of public criticism, the United Nations and member states of troop-contributing countries made little or no effort before 2003 to investigate or curb what was conventionally perceived as inevitable sexual activity by troops in the field. Indeed, in 1993, the UN Special Representative to Cambodia, Yasushi Akashi, infamously stated "boys will be boys" in response to demands for action against peacekeepers accused of abusing the people they were assigned to protect. A turning point of sorts took place in 2003 with the fist public investigation of UN peacekeepers allegedly involved in sexual exploitation.

In the last five years, there has been considerable attention paid to the issue of sexual misconduct by UN staff, international peacekeepers and humanitarian workers, the result of a call to action by human rights groups, as well as independent investigations into allegations of abuse and subsequent media exposure of the exploitation of vulnerable people in crisis settings. Fresh reports surfaced in November 2006 following a BBC investigation into more allegations of rape and underage prostitution in Liberia and Haiti. In response, the UN held a special conference in New York in early December 2006 to address the problem. At the meeting, the UN under-secretary-general for peacekeeping operations acknowledged that sexual abuse was widespread, telling reporters, "My operating presumption is that this is either a problem or a potential problem in every single one of our missions." [2]

Helen, Bunia DRC.

" BUNIA, Congo, Dec. 16 - In the corner of the tent where she says a soldier forced himself on her, Helen [pictured above], a frail fifth grader with big eyes and skinny legs, remembers seeing a blue helmet. The United Nations peacekeeper who tore off her clothes had used a cup of milk to lure her close, she said in her high-pitched voice, fidgeting as she spoke. It was her favorite drink, she said, but one her family could rarely afford. 'I was so happy,' she said. After she gulped it down, the foreign soldier pulled Helen, a 12-year-old, into bed, she said. About an hour later, he gave her a dollar, put a finger to his lips and pushed her out of his tent, she said."

(First part of a New York Times front-page article that exposed the story of sexual exploitation and rape by UN peacekeepers: In Congo War, Even Peacekeepers Add to Horror, by Marc Lacey, 18 December 2004.)

Image by Guillaume Bonn

The prediction seemed all too true as even more allegations emerged from other peacekeeping missions – this time in Sudan in early January 2007. The British newspaper The Daily Telegraph cited an internal report by the UN children's agency Unicef containing allegations of rape and sexual abuse of children by UN peacekeepers. A UN spokesperson publicly admitted on 5 January that four Bangladeshi peacekeepers had already been repatriated for sexual abuse in Sudan and 13 other staff members at the UN mission in Sudan were still being investigated.

While some analysts argue that most allegations against peacekeepers cannot be equated with the scale and terror of random, brutal and systematic rape in warfare, it is yet another context of vulnerable women and girls being abused by uniformed men in positions of power. Allegations of sexual exploitation and rape of boys and men are also evident in some cases.

Proportionally, the percentage of misconduct and abuse by civilian international staff accompanying peacekeeping missions is higher than that of military, i.e., while there are always more military than civilians in peacekeeping operations, a higher percentage of civilians are implicated in sexual abuse cases.

It is because international peacekeepers and aid workers have such an important physical and emblematic status – representing the international aspirations of human dignity, security and civilian protection – that their abuse of their position is considered, by many, so unacceptable.

Widespread and unchecked

In 2005, the 108 UN member states contributed approximately 80,000 peacekeepers, most of which were uniformed, to 17 peacekeeping missions worldwide. In situations where the vulnerable local population has been abused and is beleaguered by conflict, and where grinding poverty pervades, UN staff offer locals an increased degree of security as well as a much-needed influx of cash for goods and services. The dangerous combination of thousands of relatively well-paid young men posted overseas in environments where the rule of law and other societal constraints are often absent, with permissive troop leadership has allowed the sexual abuse and/or exploitation of local populations. In some cases, the abuse has become more widespread as the behaviour continued unchecked.

As an organisation, the UN has for some years expressed the aim of zero tolerance of abuse and zero sexual contact with local populations. However, it has been criticised for not pursuing or enforcing these aims vigorously. And many of those familiar with the cases argue that whatever allegations were made public in the Democratic Republic of Congo (DRC) in 2004 and 2005, or elsewhere, they were only the tip of the iceberg.

> **"It is, quite frankly, hard to believe that scores of allegations can emerge without being illustrative of a widespread problem. We do not know how many cases are going unreported, whether in MONUC or elsewhere."**

Jean-Marie Guéhenno, the UN's under-secretary-general for peacekeeping operations, admitted to the Special Committee on Peacekeeping Operations in New York in January 2005, "It is, quite frankly, hard to believe that scores of allegations can emerge without being illustrative of a widespread problem. We do not know how many cases are going unreported, whether in MONUC [the UN mission to the DRC] or elsewhere. In all likelihood, peacekeepers have committed acts of sexual exploitation and abuse in other missions throughout the past decade, but the vast majority has not been formally reported to headquarters. It is now apparent that neither you [member states] nor we have been aggressive enough to search for and expose these cases."

Public exposure

In November 2004, the Washington Post headlined news of confidential UN reports of sexual abuse by various staff in the DRC. At first count, approximately 150 separate allegations were being considered. The ensuing international scandal forced the UN to react publicly to the accusations and set in motion its own investigations and responses. The report suggested that soldiers from various national contingents and some civilian UN staff were involved in rape, prostitution and paedophilia.

Most of the allegations of sexual exploitation or abuse involved prostitution, while incidents of rape and sex with minors were far fewer. In some cases, there were also allegations of rape of prostitutes. All of these activities are prohibited for all UN staff. The Secretary-General's October 2003 Bulletin on Special Protection from Sexual Exploitation and Abuse, the UN Code of Conduct for Blue Helmets, and MONUC's Code of Conduct, similar to other missions' codes of conduct, are clear on this issue: Any exchange of money, employment, goods or services for sex is strictly prohibited. Furthermore, any type of sexual activity with persons under the age of 18 years is prohibited. Mistaken belief in the age of a child is not a defence or an excuse. Where substantiated, these acts warrant summary dismissal in the case of civilian staff, and repatriation and subsequent disciplinary action by member states for military and civilian police personnel.

Illustrating one of the key weaknesses in the UN's attempt to come down heavily on the guilty is the fact that it has no means or authority to bring perpetrators to justice. The UN can, and does, recommend perpetrators

Peacekeepers and other internationals who engage in transactional sex in these environments – however willing the local women may appear – are de facto exploiting the very people they are supposed to protect.

be repatriated, but it has no capacity to ensure transparent investigations or punishment. Exclusive jurisdiction is granted to the member state in whose forces the soldiers serve, in conformity with the 1946 Convention on the Privileges and Rights of the United Nations. It is therefore considered incumbent upon member states to ensure that their nationals are brought to justice. For many battalions, however, a sexual scandal during a foreign assignment would tarnish their reputation, so considerable effort is made to deal with the issue quietly, if at all.

Just prostitution?

A separate issue has been raised in Haiti and other countries with peacekeeping operations where prostitution is illegal. Peacekeepers using prostitutes, therefore, are also breaking national law while attempting to reassert the rule of law through their mission.

In the context of allegations against scores of MONUC personnel in all categories having solicited prostitutes in the DRC, Jean-Marie Guéhenno joined others seeking to debunk the idea that consorting with local prostitutes was a straightforward transaction between consenting adults: "The term 'prostitution'… can mask the exploitative nature of the dynamic. In many cases in the DRC, the so-called sex workers have been paid scraps of food, and have been girls as young as 13 and 14 years of age," he stated in early 2005.

Numerous experts on gender-based violence, observers and civil-society groups have stressed that in situations of extreme vulnerability and poverty, where women have already suffered considerable sexual abuse, there is no level playing field between peacekeepers and civilians. In

Liberia, for example, some studies suggested between 60 percent and 70 percent of women experienced physical or sexual abuse by armed combatants in the recent civil war.[3]

The reports from Haiti and DRC indicate that the extremely low payment girls and women accept for sex illustrates the desperate poverty surrounding them and the socioeconomic chasm between them and peacekeepers or other humanitarian workers. In Sierra Leone, a hierarchy in pricing of prostitutes existed: internally displaced Sierra Leonean women who had come to Freetown from the provinces and Liberian women refugees were unable to negotiate a higher price because they were poorer and more vulnerable than local women from Freetown, who could command relatively higher payments.[4]

Peacekeepers and other internationals who engage in transactional sex in these environments – however willing the local women may appear – are de facto exploiting the very people they are supposed to protect. It is on these grounds that a "zero contact" policy has been promulgated as part of the code of practice for all UN staff on assignment.

Multinational involvement

An internal UN report on allegations of abuse in the DRC obtained by the Washington Post in December 2004 indicated that those sent to investigate sexual misbehaviour in the early summer of 2004 were threatened and witnesses bribed to change incriminating testimony. "Sexual exploitation and abuse, particularly prostitution of minors, is widespread and long-standing. Moreover, all the major contingents appear to be involved," the report stated, listing contingents from Morocco, Pakistan, Nepal, Uruguay, Tunisia and South Africa.

As international outrage grew, observers and even UN officials finally acknowledged that the DRC was far from being an isolated case: similar allegations had been made in most UN missions in recent years, particularly in Haiti, Eritrea, Liberia, Cote d'Ivoire, Kosovo and Sierra Leone. Earlier allegations had also been made during missions to Cambodia and Bosnia in the early and mid-1990s. Again, human rights investigators and journalists documented widespread abuse in 2001 in Kosovo and Bosnia, where UN police operated brothels and were involved in trafficking of women from Eastern Europe to engage in prostitution. Jordanian, Palestinian and German troops were implicated in the trafficking scandal.[5]

Concerning the DRC allegations, "The situation appears to be one of 'zero-compliance with zero-tolerance' throughout the mission," stated a summary of the findings of a UN mission to the region led by Prince Zeid al-Hussein, Jordan's UN ambassador. Al-Hussein subsequently became the Secretary-General's special advisor on the issue and led the team that produced the report, A Comprehensive Strategy to Eliminate Future Exploitation and Abuse in United Nations Peacekeeping Operations, which was released in February 2005.

Must boys be boys?

Also in early 2005, the US-based advocacy agency Refugees International (RI) launched Must boys be boys? – Ending sexual exploitation and abuse in peacekeeping missions by Sarah Martin, which revealed findings of field studies carried out to gauge the scope of the problem in DRC and elsewhere.

While being critical of the behaviour and prevalence of sexual abuse amongst different UN missions, RI also recognised that around the world, the military struggles to address issues of sexual misconduct, whether on peacekeeping assignments or at home. RI also highlighted the particular "hypermasculine" culture of peacekeeping missions, which "has produced tolerance for extreme behaviours such as sexual exploitation and abuse", and the "wall of silence" in male-dominated environments, where the tendency to close ranks, resist external investigation and suppress whistle-blowers is strong.

In a report to the UN Security Council in February 2006, al-Hussein warned that continued allegations against peacekeepers would not be "entirely unexpected" until the strategy to address the problem was fully implemented.

RI suspects, however, that people have become tight-lipped and grown more likely to protect each other since the external interest and investigations began, despite the fact that the sexual abuse is widespread and common amongst troops as well as civilian UN personnel in DRC. According to RI, the prevailing opinion on the ground appears to be, Why damage a good man's career over a meaningless sexual encounter in a foreign land? Evidence from subsequent missions in Sudan and DRC suggests that some contingents now regularly host private parties, to which prostitutes are invited in order to get around the rules.

At the highest levels of the UN there appears to be considerable embarrassment, a sense of shame and a strong desire to address the problem comprehensively. There is anger, too, from members of the peacekeeping ranks and the UN who feel the good name and courage of thousands of peacekeepers are being dishonoured by a few.

Although some troop-contributing countries maintain the issue has been hyped by a few Western nations and driven by the media,[6] a recent study in Haiti found that during the 22-month period from the end of 2005 approximately 35,000 girls and women were raped or sexually assaulted in Port-au-Prince. Despite these shockingly high levels and the presence of peacekeepers, none of the respondents in the household study named a peacekeeper as having perpetrated any of these violations. They did name peacekeepers as having made violent and sexual threats, however.[7]

It appears to be clear that the going may get tougher and further allegations will emerge before things improve. A senior UN official who led a task force on sexual exploitation was quoted in 2006 as saying, "We have violated our duty of care, and we need to fix that problem. We're

> [...] the prevailing opinion on the ground appears to be, Why damage a good man's career over a meaningless sexual encounter in a foreign land?

shining our light here and it's not a pretty picture. But when you are in the swamp, the only way out of the swamp is through the swamp."

Eroding confidence

Few of those involved in the investigations underestimate the seriousness of the allegations and the impact they are having on the image of peacekeepers worldwide. In his January 2005 address to the UN Special Committee on Peacekeeping Operations, Jean-Marie Guéhenno stated, "Just as the catastrophic failure of any one operation could irreparably erode public confidence in UN peacekeeping, so, too, could acts of gross misconduct, if we do not respond to them with the utmost seriousness in 2005. We have a real substantive problem, not just a PR issue that needs to be 'spun'. We have to deal with it collectively, aggressively and quickly. And, we must prevent it from happening elsewhere."

The Secretary-General's May 2006 report on the issue confirmed a rise in investigations and allegations. The total number of 375 allegations of sexual exploitation and abuse in 2005 was far higher than the 121 allegations reported in 2004, but the rise is more likely due to higher awareness of the issue and more careful reporting. According to experts in gender-based violence programmes, there is often a rise in reporting as systems are put in place and women begin to trust the reporting mechanisms.

The UN's own figures show 316 peacekeeping personnel in all missions have been investigated, resulting in summary dismissal of 18 civilians, repatriation of 17 members of formed police units and 144 repatriations or rotations home on disciplinary grounds.[8]

The majority of all the allegations, or 340 of the total 373 allegations, were against the members of the department of peacekeeping operations. Thirty (9 percent) of these allegations involved sexual

> ### "We have a real substantive problem, not just a PR issue that needs to be 'spun'. We have to deal with it collectively, aggressively and quickly. And, we must prevent it from happening elsewhere."

assault and rape. As of May 2006, only 24 of these cases had been substantiated. A further 130 (35 percent) were deemed "unsubstantiated", and the rest are still being investigated or decided upon. These figures, which are widely suspected to be unrepresentative of a higher, real figure of the scale of sexual abuse, illustrate that even when cases are investigated, substantiating sexual crimes is difficult.

Effective response?

What then has the UN done, and in what ways has it recognised the problem and taken steps to address it?

On 31 October 2000, the UN Security Council unanimously adopted Resolution 1325 on women, peace and security. Resolution 1325 marks the first time the Security Council addressed the disproportionate and unique impact of armed conflict on women; recognised the undervalued and underutilised contributions women make in conflict prevention, peacekeeping, conflict resolution and peace-building; and stressed the importance of their equal and full participation as active agents in peace and security.

Part of Resolution 1325 called "on all parties to armed conflict to take special measures to protect women and girls from gender-based violence, particularly rape and other forms of sexual abuse" It also emphasised the

"responsibility of all States to put an end to impunity and to prosecute those responsible for genocide, crimes against humanity, war crimes including those relating to sexual violence against women and girls, and in this regard, stresses the need to exclude these crimes, where feasible from amnesty provisions."

Beyond creating codes of conduct in 1997 and again in 2001 and the inclusion of a gender and peacekeeping module within peacekeepers' deployment training, the first major reactions from the UN in relation to allegations against peacekeepers was to investigate the scope of the problem and create special committees.

The Inter-Agency Standing Committee Working Group (UN and NGOs) established in March 2002 the Task Force on Protection from Sexual Exploitation and Abuse in Humanitarian Crises – known as the IASC TF. They elaborated a plan of action in July of the same year.

In 2003, the task force supported the drafting and finalisation of the Secretary-General's Bulletin (known as the SGB) on special measures for protection from sexual exploitation and sexual abuse. The bulletin obliges all staff to report concerns or suspicions of sexual exploitation and abuse and places the onus on managers at all levels to support and develop systems to prevent sexual exploitation and abuse, including the appointment of senior staff to receive complaints. The bulletin applies to all UN staff, including separately administered organs and programmes, as well as all organisations or individuals entering into cooperative arrangements with the UN.

In February 2005, the Executive Committees on Peace and Security and on Humanitarian Affairs (ECHA) established the Task Force on Protection from Sexual Exploitation and Abuse (this followed the IASC TF), whose mandate is to follow up on the recommendations of the final report of the IASC Task Force and set certain priorities, such as developing a policy on providing support to victims of sexual exploitation and abuse by UN staff or related personnel.

In April 2005, the Special Committee on Peacekeeping Operations recommended that the Secretary-General develop "a comprehensive strategy for assistance to victims of sexual exploitation and abuse, including means for financial compensation" and further recommended that until such a strategy had been implemented, "missions should provide emergency assistance to [such] victims [...] within current

Pakistani United Nations peacekeepers on mission in troubled eastern Democratic Republic of Congo, 2005. Outgoing UN Secretary-General Kofi Annan told some 150 participants at the High Level Conference on Eliminating Sexual Exploitation and Abuse by UN and NGO Personnel in December 2006 that although significant progress had been made on the issue, "We have really only begun to tackle this egregious problem." He claimed only a small number of individuals undermined the "admirable and upstanding behaviour of the majority of United Nations staff and the uniformed personnel who serve alongside them." Civilian and military UN personnel had breached UN standards by having sex with adult prostitutes and had committed crimes such as rape, paedophilia and human trafficking, Annan said. "All of this is utterly immoral, and completely at odds with our mission. Our behaviour should be something that others can emulate, and be judged against."

Image: Brent Stirton

mission budgets." This recommendation was endorsed by the General Assembly in June 2005.

In the 2005 World Summit Outcome, member states again encouraged the Secretary-General to "submit proposals to the General Assembly leading to a comprehensive approach to victims' assistance by 31 December 2005."

In March 2005, the much-cited Zeid Report came out with specific recommendations. The report was a culmination of the IASC and ECHA task forces and drew on experience in all peacekeeping operations. It focused on a comprehensive, four-pronged strategy: establishing more stringent rules and regulations concerning sexual conduct; improving the investigative process; demanding more from command and management responsibility; and, lastly, implementing individual discipline and criminal accountability. Special budgets were dedicated to overseeing the implementation of this new strategy three months later, and the strategy is currently being put into operation.

Refugees International endorsed and approved Zeid's recommendations. In their Must Boys be Boys? report, they also outline a series of recommendations, including systematically incorporating a gender perspective into all UN peacekeeping missions; establishing culturally appropriate predeployment training; changing attitudes of senior management and holding them accountable for failure to implement measures to stop sexual exploitation and abuse; improving access to the UN complaint system; and providing women with economic opportunities so they have the means to support themselves and their families.

Many analysts say that having more female peacekeepers would help address the problem. Sarah Martin has pointed out that this would be difficult to achieve in a timely fashion, since according to 2004 UN statistics, only 4.4 percent of civilian police are women. Currently, 1 percent of peacekeeping troops and 27 percent of UN civilian personnel are women. Most of the countries that contribute troops do not have large numbers of women in their forces. More important is focusing on changing the culture that has allowed sexual exploitation and abuse to flourish.

Changing attitudes

Anna Shotton, the Focal Point for Sexual Exploitation and Abuse for the UN Department of Peacekeeping Operations, claimed in late 2005 that the department had made "tremendous progress" and had implemented a number of measures to address the problem, including training programmes, recreational sports facilities and public-information campaigns to "push the message home at every opportunity." Still, she agreed that the message had "not taken hold", despite the firing of 10 civilian employees and the repatriation of 88 soldiers following 221 separate investigations worldwide during 2004 and 2005.

According to the British medical journal The Lancet, "Since 2004, only 17 peacekeepers have been dismissed and 161 repatriated out of 313 allegations worldwide."[9]

The UN and its troop-contributing countries must go further to ensure that peacekeepers understand why the rules are in place. "You cannot rule by fear alone," Martin argued, claiming that peacekeepers would only find ways around the UN's rules unless they agreed that it was important not to take advantage of a population traumatised by conflict.

Referring to the low number of successful investigations into abuse allegations, Guéhenno told the member states in early 2005, "We need your help to address obvious shortcomings in our investigative capacities. Proving sex crimes is one of the most difficult prosecutorial challenges for even the most sophisticated criminal justice systems, let alone for peacekeeping operations, which, at present, are woefully ill-equipped to investigate them."

He concluded by saying, "This is more than a loose end. It is more than a minor setback. Let me be clear. If we do not tackle this problem as one of our highest priorities in 2005, then the damage to the image and reputation of UN peacekeeping could be irreparable."

A sobering conclusion ends the RI study, with Martin claiming, "Every SRSG [Special Representative of the Secretary General] and military commander has a 'zero tolerance' policy when it comes to sexual exploitation and abuse, but without the ability to actually implement these recommendations, zero tolerance is meaningless." Without this

One of many commercial sex workers looking for clients at a popular nightspot in Sierra Leone. Some of the thousands of these women claim that UN personnel and international aid workers are vital clients in their struggle to survive in the post-war context. Saying that there is also a "supply side" to sexual exploitation and abuse, Jasmine Whitebread, chief executive of Save the Children - UK, stated in December 2006 that organisations in the field need to "make sure that selling her body is not the only way a young girl can feed herself or her family." These organisations must address the issue of entrenched poverty, she said, and the "inability of families to make a sufficient living after a crisis is over."

Image: Brent Stirton

ability to implement recommendations, and without the requisite political will by troop-contributing countries and the UN itself, it is likely to be a long, slow journey to end sexual impunity in peacekeeping missions and see stricter punishments for those who transgress. In the meantime, women, girls and boys will continue to be abused and exploited, in some cases, by the very people sent to protect them, and the UN and its peacekeepers will bear the stain as more cases are exposed and publicised.

Aid Workers:
"The children will have sex with him to get the food"[10]

"If I tell you the name of the NGO worker I have to sex with [sic], he will get fired, and then how will I feed my child and myself?" a young mother in Guinea asked interviewers in 2003, as more and more evidence of sexual exploitation by staff from local and international nongovernmental organisations in West Africa emerged.
In early 2002, a sex scandal broke out over a suppressed, but leaked, report that indicated humanitarian workers were using their position to

The investigative team discovered a widespread and "possibly endemic" culture of exploitation.

obtain sex from young refugee girls in West Africa. The subsequent furore in the international aid community and rush to investigate further afield suggested that such behaviour was not confined to West Africa.

A joint investigation into abuse allegations involving national and international aid workers in three West African countries by the United Nations High Commissioner for Refugees (UNHCR) and Save the Children-UK (SCF-UK) was completed in late 2001. A preliminary report on the investigation was leaked ahead of the report's official release date in late February 2002 because of the disturbing nature of the allegations and the apparent scope of the problem. This leak revealed accusations by children against 67 named aid workers from more than 40 agencies, including UN peacekeepers and community leaders. The children, mainly girls, in refugee camps in Liberia, Guinea and Sierra Leone said they had traded sexual favours for shelter, education and medicine.

Paul Nolan, child protection manager for SCF-UK, said at that time the investigative team discovered a widespread and "possibly endemic" culture of exploitation. Nolan was quoted as saying, "It's a problem we

know has been around for some time. There have been abuses in the past. What this does is show, in very stark terms, in the words of children themselves, the kinds of experiences they are being subjected to."[11]

"In this community, no one can access CSB [a soya nutrient] without having sex first. They say: 'A kilo for sex'," a refugee woman in Guinea told the interviewers. At a different camp, in Sierra Leone, one man said: "If you do not have a wife or a sister or a daughter to offer the NGO workers, it is hard to have access to aid."[12]

"It's difficult to escape the trap of those people; they use the food as bait to get you to sex with them," an adolescent in Liberia told interviewers from the UNHCR and SCF-UK. Reports of these investigations also quoted refugee leaders in Guinea as saying, "If you see a young girl walking away with [a] tarpaulin on her head, you know how she got it."

In testimonies, taken mainly from girls under age 18, many girls talked about exchanging sexual favours for food, saying they did not realise they were entitled to the rations without conditions. Others said they negotiated sex for shelter, education and medicine. Most of the alleged abusers were male national staff who targeted girls.

According to the report, "The kids are in a desperate situation. In order to survive, they have to make the choice between going without food or selling themselves, the only currency they have left to them. [...] It's a problem that cuts across the whole of the sector."[13]

The report, which said the problem was worst in places that had well-established aid programmes, said the children's allegations could not be independently verified. Despite calls by governments and NGOs to provide on a confidential basis the names of the individuals alleged to have taken part, UNHCR and SCF-UK declined, citing "legal concerns and fairness," as well as the limitations of anecdotal information.

The reluctance of the two agencies to reveal the details appalled many agencies and governments at the time who complained that not only were they unable to discipline staff or change internal procedures, but that perpetrators might continue to commit such crimes if left unpunished. UNHCR, however, insisted that furnishing the names might put child victims still living in camps at risk. The organisation was prepared to reveal confidentially which agencies and NGOs were implicated, but not the names of individuals accused of perpetrating the abuse.

Food distribution at camps for displaced people in northern Uganda. Approximately 1.5 million people in 200 camps continue to seek shelter from the insecurity and violence instigated by the Lord's Resistance Army. Aid workers throughout the world often work with the most vulnerable and disenfranchised communities. In some cases, they offer the only hope for shelter, water, food and medical assistance in conflict and post-conflict situations. This position of trust can easily be abused for personal gain. According to investigative reports in recent years, that position of trust frequently has been, and continues to be, abused for sexual gratification and control over women and girls.

Images: Sven Torfinn / OCHA

Subsequent investigations by the UN claimed to have found many of the allegations unsubstantiated and the testimonies "vague and unconvincing", which again indicates the difficulty of securing hard evidence in these cases. It may also indicate the difficulties refugee children, without resources or power, face when making accusations against adults in positions of power, particularly when those adults are part of international agencies desperate to avoid any public scandal. Despite the limitations of the evidence in 2002, both UNHCR and SCF-UK stated, " [...] the number of allegations leaves no doubt that there is a serious problem of sexual exploitation."[14]

Following the exposure of the potential scale of the problem in 2002, UN agencies and NGOs have moved to develop codes of conduct, strict guidelines, training manuals and more effective avenues for complaints against their workers in regard to sexual exploitation and abuse. In Sierra Leone, local and international NGOs, UN agencies and some government bodies collaborated through the interagency Co-ordinating Committee for the Prevention of Sexual Exploitation and Abuse (CCSEA). Training is a key component in CCSEA's strategy to ensure that all relief and development workers are educated about the need to prevent sexual abuse and exploitation and have a common understanding of standards of behaviour. Agencies believe that maintaining an ongoing dialogue on sexual abuse and exploitation through participation on the CCSEA also helps to promote accountability and sharing information.

Critics and observers, however, say sexual abuse and exploitation is deeply rooted in gender-related power dynamics and cannot be addressed solely through codes of conduct and training programmes. Understanding gender inequalities and the way in which they make people vulnerable to sexual abuse and exploitation must be an essential part of all efforts to prevent it, they maintain. Furthermore, some cynics said the agencies' activism in pursuing this agenda is closely linked to detrimental publicity such as that of 2002, and as media interest wanes, so, too, will the commitment to enforce these standards.

Some donors have taken an active role in requiring their implementing partners to be more vigilant. As a result of fears of sexual exploitation of orphaned children following the 2004 tsunami disaster, the US Congress passed a law requiring any organisation funded by the US Agency for International Development (USAID) to have codes of conduct in place regarding sexual exploitation and abuse. By making this as a condition of funding, advocates hoped it would lead NGOs that had not yet revamped their organisations to initiate training on sexual exploitation and abuse. Nevertheless, some observers said that at this point, only some of the major international NGOs have adopted rigorous codes of conduct.

The UN promised to put safeguards in place when sexual abuse in the refugee camps of West Africa was first revealed in 2002, but it is not clear if progress has been made. In March 2006, fresh reports circulated from SCF-UK that Liberian girls as young as age eight were still being sexually exploited by aid workers and peacekeepers despite pledges to stamp out such abuse.

SCF-UK's study, which involved interviewing more than 300 people in camps for war-displaced, revealed that those who were questioned claimed that more than half of the girls where they live, between the ages of eight and 18, were being "sold for sex".[15] In response, the UN in Liberia said it would investigate specific allegations.

This brief report on the scandal of humanitarian aid workers sexually exploiting and abusing those they are supposed to help is not directly related to rape and sexual abuse during times of war. However, it pertains to the issue of uniformed peacekeepers and civilian humanitarian staff exploiting people placed under their care for humanitarian protection and sustenance. Normally, this occurs during conflict or during peace negotiations and in post-conflict environments, where local populations are poor and vulnerable. Because the issue is related to female sexual vulnerability in and around conflict, it has been included in this publication. ■

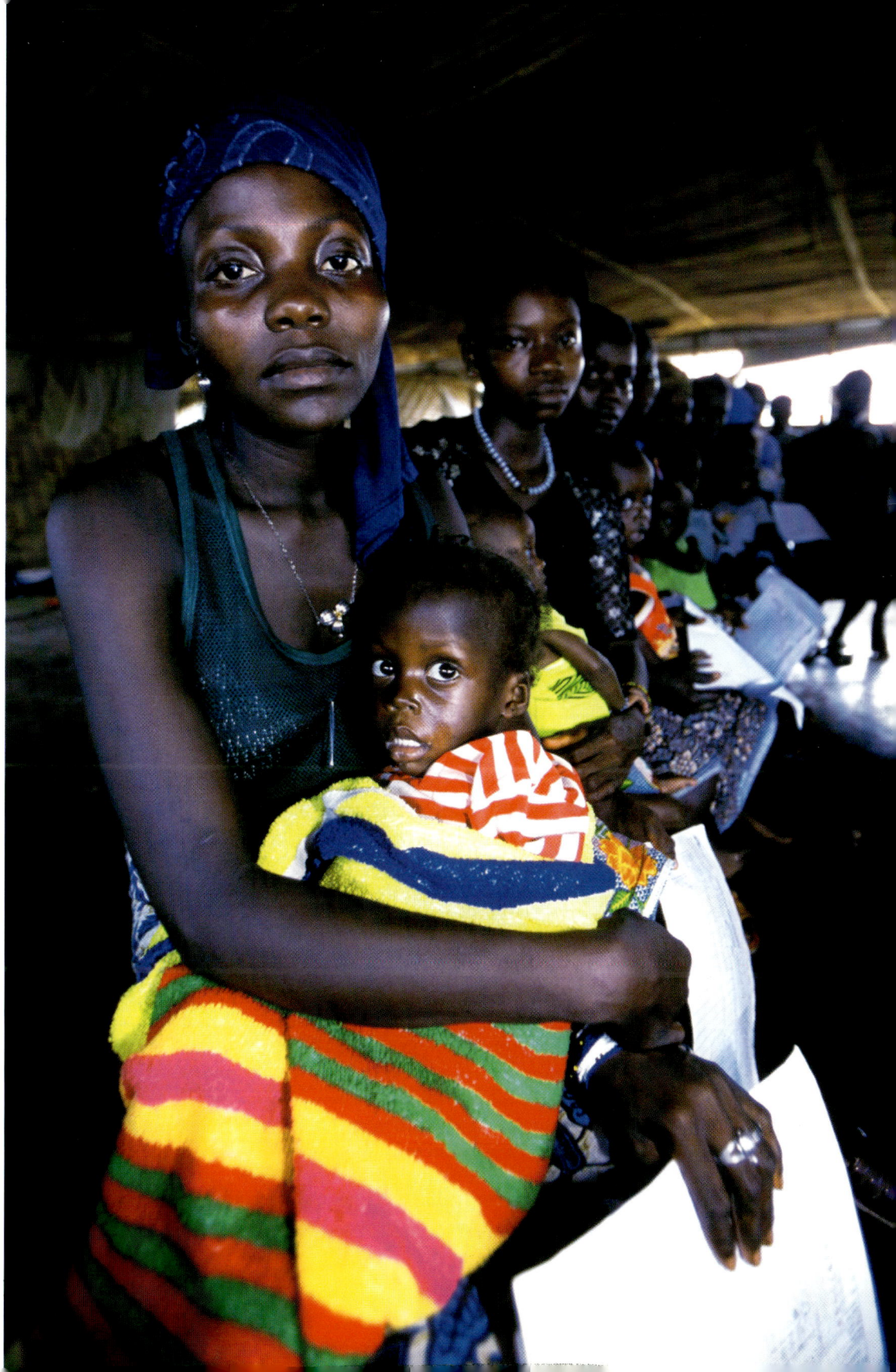

Those in refugee or IDP camps around the world, are entirely dependant on local authorities and more specifically aid workers for their food, shelter, water and health. In many cases women and children are alone in camps without male partners to protect them from sexual exploitation.

Image: Brent Stirton

"Elizabeth" and her four-year-old daughter were brutally raped and beaten by six militiamen near their home in Masisi, Democratic Republic of Congo. Her daughter was carried away by their attackers, and the baby son that Elizabeth was carrying on her back throughout the assault subsequently died. Through counselling provided by Doctors On Call Services (DOCS), Elizabeth has been able to begin the healing process.

"I am now ready to talk about my story. Before I was raped, both my parents were killed in the war, as were many of my relatives. In fact, my three sisters are widows because their husbands were all killed.

One morning in November 2004 I went to look for food in the field with two of my children. My four-year-old daughter and I were carrying baskets, but my son was just a baby so I had him on my back. We were going to our *shamba* [fruit and vegetable garden] 15 kilometres away to look for bananas, plaintain and pineapple, when the militiamen appeared in front of and behind us. The six men pushed us from the path to the nearest field and tied my daughter's and my arms behind our backs. They started to beat us with their guns, and also beat and kicked my baby. I still suffer from intense pain now, even if I carry the smallest bucket.

As they were beating me, I fell to the ground with my baby still on my back. It was then that they took off my skirt and began raping me, with my baby on my back throughout. It was impossible to resist — we couldn't even make any noise. I was raped by three men and my daughter was raped by the other three at the same time, lying next to me on the ground. While one raped each of us, the other two would point their guns and hold us down with their feet. When one finished, the next would start. I felt totally useless — there was no way to shout as they would have killed us. When it was over, they took my daughter away with them. I have not seen her since.

I had such terrible pains in my stomach, vagina and back that they had left thinking I was dead. I could only crawl, and crawled through the bush for three days. They had taken everything I had, so I was completely naked. I put leaves on my body, and carried my baby, who was very sick. He had been beaten badly and when I fell to the ground I had landed on him. He died a week after the attack.

Some people passed me in the bush and I sent them to fetch my sister. She took me back to Masisi, where I found that my house had been looted the same day that I was raped. Everything had been taken. My husband, who had married again and was living in Mweso with his new wife, and I had been friends, but after the rape he rejected me entirely.

Through my sister I met the counsellors [affiliated to DOCS] who helped me. I was taken to hospital a week after the attack, where they told me that my stomach was damaged. I was unable to walk, so I was sent home, and I am now waiting until I am strong enough to travel to DOCS. They wouldn't let me travel before, as my condition was so bad that they thought I might die on the way. I am getting stronger but my back is still very bad.

I used to go to our *shamba* every day, but my back was so damaged by the beating and the rape that I can't anymore — I just don't have the strength. I am also too scared to go. Sometimes I have nightmares and can't sleep. At other times I wake up and lose all hope, as I have been dreaming of dying. Support from my community has helped me, as has my faith in God. DOCS came to counsel us — they gave us hope and encouraged us to continue living.

"DOCS has also given me a goat, beans and a hoe. I am so happy — it proves to me that I am loved. I live with my six children and had to beg for food as before today I didn't have the materials for working. We are so poor, my children can't go to school. But I am going to rear the goat and grow the beans for food."

Images: Georgina Cranston

A self-help group of women in Sierra Leone – all survivors of sexual violence and torture. They posed for this photo wanting the world to know of their needs and the abuse they suffered. Thousands of women like them struggle to find a future, let alone justice, after living through years of brutal conflict.

Image: Brent Stirton

seeking post-conflict justice

"Rapid establishment by the United Nations of interim judicial systems capable of dealing effectively with violations against women by family members and society at large. Rape and sexual violence should be addressed by post-conflict truth- and justice-seeking mechanisms at national and local levels. The treatment of crimes against women in traditional mechanisms should be consistent with international standards."

One of the clusters of recommendation from the independent experts' assessment on the impact of armed conflict on women and women's role in peace-building, titled Women, War and Peace.

A number of mechanisms are increasingly being used to provide some level of justice for victims of sexual violence during conflict and to ensure accountability for crimes committed. These can be carried out at national, international and regional levels, using a variety of judicial methods including national courts, *ad hoc* tribunals, hybrid and international courts.[1] Nonjudicial methods, such as truth commissions, are also increasingly being used.

Despite these efforts, however, the inescapable truth is that rape and sexual violence are routinely used as part of the military arsenal to demoralise, terrorise and humiliate civilians and that perpetrators continue to enjoy near total impunity.[2] Alternatively, or in addition, these crimes are perpetrated as part of the rapacious sexual opportunism of ill-disciplined and brutal fighting forces.

Indeed, the deliberate targeting of women continues into post-conflict periods, where criminal activity often thrives and the rule of law is weak or nonexistent.[3] Even after peace agreements are signed, women and girls continue to be exposed to increased levels of rape and sexual violence in their homes, refugee camps and on the streets at the hands of their families, law-enforcement officers, returning combatants, the military, police and even peacekeeping forces,[4] with little being done to address their plight.

Testimonies and research from refugee camps, such as those for Rwandans in Tanzania, and internally displaced people's sites in Darfur, Sudan, or Colombia, or from towns and villages in northeastern Democratic Republic of Congo, Iraq and Sri Lanka, point to pervasive and unending sexual violence against women in areas of weak

A 13-year-old girl, raped by armed men, waits for treatment in a health clinic in Goma, eastern Democratic Republic of Congo, August 2006. During five years of armed conflict in the DRC, tens of thousands of women and girls have suffered crimes of sexual violence such as gang rape, mutilations and abduction by combatants for long periods of sexual slavery. How will reparations or restitutions ever be given to these victims and when will perpetrators of these crimes be held accountable for their careless brutality?

Image: Tiggy Ridley

governance. Even where social control is exerted and enforced, if a predominance of undisciplined military personnel are in close contact with civilian communities, rape and sexual abuse continue.

Participants at a 2006 high-level international conference in Brussels on sexual violence in conflict concluded they were "deeply concerned that the response to sexual violence in conflict and beyond is grossly inadequate when compared to the scope of the phenomenon and agree with the report of the independent expertson women, war and peace [Rehn and Johnson-Sirleaf, 2002] that the standards of protection for women affected by conflict are glaring in their inadequacy, as is the international response."[5]

According to Binaifer Nowrojee, lawyer and researcher at Human Rights Watch and member of the Coalition for Women's Human Rights in Conflict Situations, "Historically, there has been a silence surrounding the sex crimes against women that downplays their suffering and renders them invisible. Sexual violence is often dismissed as the private act of a combatant or an unfortunate by-product of war."[6]

Numerous obstacles prevent women from seeking justice: Legal aid is rarely available to them, and gender bias in national judicial systems – the very systems that are supposed to protect them – may prevent women from receiving fair treatment as witnesses and victims.[7] Indeed, women are often blamed for sexual crimes visited upon them and risk retribution, stigmatisation and rejection by their families and communities for pursuing justice.

According to Human Rights Watch, women's subordinate status in many societies directly contributes to both a heightened risk of victimisation during conflict, as well as inadequate institutional responses to it post-conflict.[8] In Sierra Leone, for example, women face widespread discrimination in practice, law and custom. Provisions in the constitution contain a guarantee of sexual equality alongside discriminatory clauses on adoption, marriage, divorce, inheritance and other areas. Under customary and Islamic law – the two systems under which most women marry – women have subordinate status and are often considered legal minors. Under customary law, a wife can only refuse to have sexual intercourse with her husband if she is physically ill, menstruating or breast-feeding. In addition, she may refuse sex during the day, in the bush or during Ramadan. Domestic violence is commonplace: A man has a right to "reasonably chastise his wife by physical force" under customary law. In some communities, only rape of a virgin is considered a serious crime. Even then, punishment for rape in local courts often involves fining the perpetrator, with a sum of money paid to the victim's family for the loss of her honour.

> "Historically, there has been a silence surrounding the sex crimes against women that downplays their suffering and renders them invisible. Sexual violence is often dismissed as the private act of a combatant or an unfortunate by-product of war."

During Sierra Leone's civil war, where the frequency and extent of sexual violence against women reached a staggering level,[9] combatants routinely abducted women, forcing them to cook, clean and be available sexually as their "wives".

"Such relationships, of course, mimic relationships during peacetime, especially peacetime situations in which forced marriage and expectations of free female labour are common practice," LaShawn R Jefferson wrote in a study of the phenomenon for Human Rights Watch. "Men who were accustomed to exercise control over women's bodies in times of peace continued to do so with extreme brutality during the civil war."[10]

Obtaining indictments for crimes against women is most difficult at the national level, where justice systems may lack financial and human resources.[11] Legal personnel may also suffer from religious or ethnic bias resulting from the conflict.[12] A widely endorsed study on justice mechanisms concluded that investigations at this level rarely focused on violations against women, and where they did, the lack of technical capacities, legal expertise on women's rights and the absence of procedures for forensic investigations hampered prosecutions.[13] "Too often, national courts discriminate against women, detaining them without due process, dismissing their testimony and subjecting them to public humiliation," the study said. The example of Sierra Leone illustrate the shortfalls and inadequacies facing many countries in conflict or emerging from conflict where sexual abuses continue and where official / legal protection is weak.

Binaifer Nowrojee, for The Coalition for Women's Human Rights in Conflict Situations[14] said that even in international and hybrid courts the extent to which sexual crimes are included in indictments often remains dependent on the individual interest and commitment of investigators and prosecutors, rather than institutional policy.[15] This has resulted in sexual violence charges not always being brought by international prosecutors, even when evidence has been readily available. When charges are brought, they "are often added belatedly, as an afterthought, in amendments that are not properly integrated into cases."[16] In other cases, women witnesses have withdrawn from its tribunals because they were not provided with adequate support and protection.[17]

Prosecuting sexual crimes

Nowrojee has put forward a model of best practice for international prosecutors and investigators.[18]

1. **Prosecutors must have the political will to prosecute sexual violence**
   Prosecution of sexual offenders must be made a priority from the beginning by a prosecutor and senior staff, so that detailed strategies can be worked out and a unified approach adopted. Strategies must include a comprehensive analysis of the nature of the charges. Is rape to be approached as a crime against humanity, war crime or genocide? Will other forms of sexual violence be charged? Are rape charges being brought consistently against all factions/armed groups?

2. **A prosecution strategy on sexual violence must be designed at the start**
   A clear prosecution strategy ensures that the type and quality of evidence required is gathered from the beginning. Investigators require clear direction from senior prosecutors, as different strategies will require different approaches and evidentiary standards.

3. **Training must be provided for all staff**
   Training for legal staff in key areas such as investigating sexual violence, interviewing victims, relevant international legal standards and jurisprudential advances on gender-based violence is key. Lawyers beginning work with international and hybrid tribunals come with a wide variety of criminal law backgrounds and some have no experience prosecuting sexual violence.

4. **Dedicated and specialised staff must be provided**
   Having a dedicated and experienced team of investigators and prosecutors for sexual crimes, including female staff, can help to bolster attention to the issue.

5. **The wellbeing, dignity and safety of victims and witnesses must be protected**
   Courts must ensure that the victims' wellbeing is prioritised by

providing the following:
- Outreach programmes that ensure information about the work of the court reaches victims and witnesses, including those in rural areas;
- Information to victims and witnesses about the benefits and risks of giving evidence. Issues surrounding confidentiality are key. Witnesses are often guaranteed that their identities will be kept confidential, given a pseudonym and are allowed to testify behind a curtain. However, due process mostly requires that the defence be given the name of the alleged victim, often leading to leaks of identity and devastating circumstances for the victim/witness. Explicit warnings should be given to witnesses in advance to facilitate an informed decision;
- Preparation of victims by investigators and lawyers for detailed questioning about sexual acts and body parts, which often remain taboo areas of discussion;
- Access to counselling services, medical care and related health services for victims;
- Protection for witnesses during and after trials.
- Courtrooms must be enabling environments
- Judges must create an empathetic environment in which victims are treated with care, sensitivity and respect. They should intervene if cross-examination techniques are excessive, inappropriate or demeaning.

The United Nations Special Court for Sierra Leone has received much praise for its approach to sexual violence under the direction of prosecutor David Crane.[19] A lawyer was specifically tasked with developing a prosecution plan governing sexual crimes, which led to a prosecution strategy incorporating sexual violence from the start. Two out of 10 investigators at the court were also dedicated to sexual assault investigations from the beginning, resulting in 75 percent of indictments after the first year, including sexual violence charges.[20]

"Having two experienced female investigators on staff ensured the prosecutors' interviewing methodology and environment were conducive to making rape victims feel comfortable enough to recount their experiences," said a study of the court.[21]

Truth commissions as a form of recognition and justice

Truth commissions are temporary investigative bodies, officially sanctioned and established in an effort to expose and address an earlier period of repression, conflict, atrocity or systematic human rights abuse. As such, through extensive interviews, statements from experts and

Non-uniformed and uniformed armed men force a young girl out of her home during an alleged security mission in Baghdad. Currently in Iraq, a proliferation of official and unofficial armed groups wield power at gunpoint, and legitimate security units and military share de facto authority with insurgents, criminals and gangs. Human rights groups are increasingly concerned about the situation for women and girls, having seen a rise in the number of sexual attacks, disappearances, abductions and kidnappings. What recourse to protection, assistance or justice can these women appeal?

Image: Brent Stirton

A woman amputee in Sierra Leone, one of the 100,000 people brutally mutilated by the rebel Revolutionary United Front (RUF) during its attempt to terrorise communities and prevent people from voting by "cutting off the hands that vote". Part of the rebel leader Charles Taylor's destructive legacy in West Africa, his victims may take some cold comfort that he, at least, is behind bars in The Hague, awaiting trial. However, most of his foot-soldiers, his rapists and executioners, like those of many other armed factions during the war, have escaped indictment, trial or any process of justice. Despite the success of the Special Court's Truth and Reconciliation Commission in Sierra Leone, most perpetrators remain free and most victims remain poor, raising questions about the limits of transitional justice.

Image: Brent Stirton

testimonies they are increasingly illuminating the extent of sexual violence to a level of detail and importance that was previously unheard of. As nonjudicial bodies that exist for a predetermined period of time, they are best understood as a complementary strategy for addressing legacies of abuse and violence. At the close of a commission, a report of their findings is generally produced with conclusions and recommendations for future reforms.

Peace agreements increasingly include proposals for truth commissions to help process the trauma of past conflict. New governments and civil society organisations propose truth commissions in the hope that a commission will identify patterns of abuse, create new forms of reconciliation, give voice to victims and/or make strong recommendations for institutional reforms and improvements. These include prosecuting perpetrators in criminal proceedings; establishing reparations programmes (including compensation) for victims and survivors; and engaging in projects to honour the memory of victims or establish public debate about the past.

As such they are also used as a tool for legitimising the moral authority of new regimes. They only have life, however, if the political will exists to implement the recommendations and follow through on the findings. Today, truth commissions seem to be proliferating. They have gone by a variety of names, including the National Commission on the Disappearance of Persons (Argentina), National Commission on Truth and Reconciliation (Chile), National Reconciliation Commission (Ghana), Commission for Historical Clarification (Guatemala), Commission for Reception, Truth and Reconciliation (Timor-Leste), and Truth and Reconciliation Commission (Peru, Sierra Leone, South Africa).[22]

In a study drawing on the experiences of more than 30 truth commissions from the past three decades, the UN Office of the High Commissioner for Human Rights (OHCHR), reaffirmed the right for people to know the truth about human rights abuses visited on their communities, which in turn has been affirmed by regional courts, international and domestic tribunals.[23] According to OHCHR, the question of why certain events happened can be just as important as what happened, helping "a society understand and acknowledge a contested or denied history, and in doing so bring the voices and stories of victims, often hidden from public view, to the public stage."[24]

For example, the Truth and Reconciliation Commission for Sierra Leone was mandated by the Lomé Peace Accord to create an impartial record of human rights abuses that occurred there between 1991 and 1999. The subsequent Truth and Reconciliation Act described the commission as an independent institution mandated to "address impunity, to respond to the needs of the victims, to promote healing and reconciliation, and to prevent a repetition of the violations and abuses suffered."[25]

Notably, while testimonies in courts have to be confined to facts that are legally relevant, truth commissions can provide a more comprehensive understanding of patterns of violations.[26] They can also permit victims and perpetrators to recount their experiences in an uninterrupted narrative without being subjected to cross examination. Truth commissions, therefore, can serve as cathartic fora for investigating the extent of sexual abuse, especially where they are explicitly mandated to examine it. Commissions in Sierra Leone and Haiti, for example, called for specific attention to be given to victims of sexual violence.

In order to facilitate this process, OHCHR suggested that truth commissions hold women-only hearings with female commissioners and observers and allow women to testify at public hearings with their identities concealed.[27]

While the relationship between simultaneous truth commissions and court proceedings can be problematic, commissions can act as complementary justice mechanisms by recommending in their final

> **Truth commissions, therefore, can serve as cathartic fora for investigating the extent of sexual abuse, especially where they are explicitly mandated to examine it.**

reports that criminal prosecutions take place and turning over evidence to prosecuting authorities for further action.[28]

Where they may be seen to fall short, according to OHCHR, is in their inability to provide a fora for individual experiences on a case-by-case basis, which is often wished for by victims.[29] Time and financial constraints mean that at most, they are able to "provide a global truth, a description of patterns," [30] with individual cases representing countless others.

The case of Timor-Leste

Timor-Leste is an instructive example of responding to the needs of victims, their need for national and international recognition, respect and compensation. In particular, the example of Timor-Leste shows how commissions of inquiry and of truth and reconciliation can support and empower women and girls who are victims of sexual violence. However, the current situation in Timor-Leste also illustrates the political limits of commissions of this kind.

In 1975, following the end of nearly 400 years of Portuguese colonisation, Indonesia invaded Timor-Leste and brutally occupied the territory for more than 24 years. In 1999, a year after the fall of Indonesia's General Suharto, the UN administered a popular consultation where the people voted overwhelmingly for independence: 78 percent of registered voters, who themselves represented 99 percent of the population. This event was followed by weeks of intense violence and destruction by Indonesian security forces and their militia. Because the men had fled to the mountains, the women were targeted for sexual assault in a cruel and systematic way. While the militia refrained in general from killing women, they subjected them to humiliation and different forms of harassment including stripping and sexual slavery as well as rape and sexual violence. Women and children were also victims of forced displacement into exile.

An international peacekeeping force also entered Timor-Leste in September 1999 amidst violence and ongoing, serious human rights violations as Indonesia and its armed militia continued to destroy the land they had been

"The number of victims who wished to testify to the Commission became overwhelming. [...] Victims and witnesses came to testify despite living amidst destruction and despite their lack of food and other basic needs."

force to leave. A month later, the UN became the transitional administrator of the territory until its full independence on 20 May 2002.

The violence that followed the announcement of the results of the popular consultation led to the establishment of the International Commission of Inquiry on East Timor. The commission derived its mandate from the UN Commission on Human Rights Resolution S-4/1999/1 in late September 1999. The mandate was "to gather and compile systematically information on possible violations of human rights acts which might constitute breaches of international humanitarian law committed in East Timor, and to provide the Secretary-General with its conclusions with a view to enabling him to make recommendations on future actions."[31]

The International Commission of Inquiry

The primary objective of the International Commission of Inquiry was

fact-finding and information-gathering. It spent considerable time listening to testimonies provided by victims and witnesses, particularly those who had witnessed events directly. The commission gave special attention to testimonies from women victims, it claimed.

According to the commission's report, "the number of victims who wished to testify to the Commission became overwhelming. [...] Victims and witnesses came to testify despite living amidst destruction and despite their lack of food and other basic needs. Most of them came on foot, since there was total lack of transport. [...] The members of the International Commission of Inquiry were confronted with testimonies surpassing their imagination."[32]

The commission heard numerous cases of rape and sexual abuse but in total was only able to collect 170 witness statements of all kinds of violence and breaches of human rights in its nine-day visit. "Several women who had gone through the trauma of rape and sexual abuse came to narrate their bitter experiences. Some of the raped women are now faced with unwanted pregnancies. It should be noted that suffering and Commission."[33]

The subsequent recommendations of the International Commission of Inquiry recommended inter alia the establishment of an appropriate mechanism for ensuring justice and reconciliation and specifically an international independent investigation and prosecution body as well as an international human rights tribunal. In 2000, two institutions were established to assist justice and reconciliation: a specific legal instrument to hear cases and try abuses, and a truth and reconciliation commission.

The Serious Crimes Panels

In March 2000, the UN Transitional Authority for East Timor created a judicial system for the area and promulgated a regulation that set up a system of district courts, including the Serious Crimes Panels. The regulation gave the Dili District Court exclusive jurisdiction over genocide, war crimes, crimes against humanity, murder, sexual offences and torture for crimes committed between January and October 1999.

Despite good promises and according to critics within the human rights community, justice made little progress in Timor-Leste. Due to a lack of political and financial support, the UN-supported tribunal shut down in May 2005, five years after it was established. Although the tribunal did

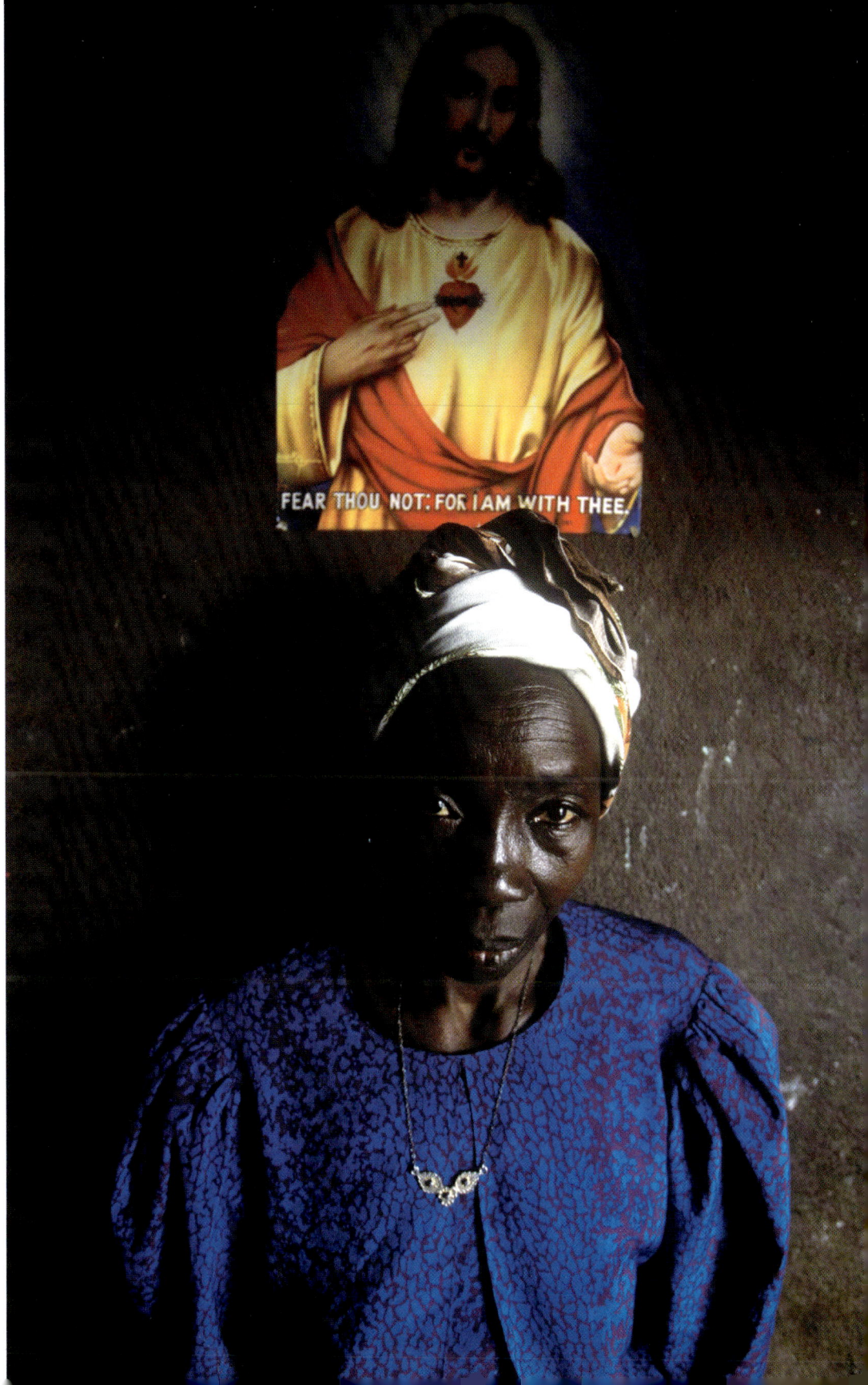

Yet another victim of rape and sexual violence in Sierra Leone. A new rise in religious devotion has followed the end of war in recent years. Observers say this is a reflection of the need for hope in a world where victims of extreme violence and social dislocation have lost faith in human systems and government which, even with the best intentions, can offer them neither material assistance, reparations nor true justice.

Image: Brent Stirton

...the intention was not only limited to the personal gratification of perpetrators or the direct impact on individual victims. The purpose was also to humiliate and dehumanise the East Timorese people.

manage to prosecute and convict a significant number of militia members, the majority of the Indonesians indicted — including General Wiranto, former Indonesian defence minister and armed forces commander — remained at large in Indonesia with no prospect of trial. Some critics concluded that both the UN Security Council and then-UN Secretary-General Kofi Annan caved in to Indonesia as a regional power and, after the events of 9/11, an important counterterrorism ally.

The Commission for Reception, Truth and Reconciliation in East-Timor

The Commission for Reception, Truth and Reconciliation in East Timor (more commonly known by its Portuguese acronym CAVR, Comissão de Acolhimento, Verdade e Reconciliação de Timor-Leste) is a body established in 2000 by the UN and the government of Timor-Leste to "inquire into human rights violations committed on all sides, between April 1974 and October 1999, and facilitate community reconciliation with justice for those who committed less serious offenses." Its mandate was far wider in terms of the time-scale than the initial UN International Commission of Inquiry.

The CAVR delivered its 2,500-page report, entitled Chega!, meaning "stop" or "enough" in Portuguese, to the president of Timor-Leste on 31 October 2005. The president then handed the report to the Secretary-General of the UN, as required by law, on 20 January 2006. As required by its legal mandate, the commission developed a gender-sensitive approach in seeking the truth about human rights violations during the political conflict. According to its final report, "Rape, sexual slavery and sexual violence were tools used as part of the campaign designed to inflict a deep experience of terror, powerlessness and hopelessness upon pro-independence supporters. Sexual violence of East Timorese women was intentionally carried out to destroy the self-esteem and spirit, not only of the victims, but of all who supported the movement for independence, with the aim of forcing them to accept the political goal of integration with Indonesia."[34]

The commission found that in addition to rape, gang rape, public rape, sexual torture and sexual slavery, a wide variety of other sexual violations were committed by members of the Indonesian security forces. Prisoners were forced to walk long distances through communities while naked, and women were tortured in military posts where other prisoners could hear their screams. This sexual torture often included mutilation of women's sexual organs, inserting of objects into vaginas, burning nipples and genitals with cigarettes, use of electric shocks applied to the genitals, breasts and mouths, forcing detainees to engage in sexual acts, rape of pregnant women, rape of women while blindfolded with their hands and feet bound, and the use of snakes to instil terror in victims. The report stated that, the scope and nature of the violations demonstrate that the intention was not only limited to the personal gratification of perpetrators or the direct impact on individual victims. The purpose was also to humiliate and dehumanise the East Timorese people.[35]

The findings are noteworthy for their focus on sexual violations and their explicit details and documentation of individuals involved in the crimes documented. Eight hundred and fifty-three cases of rape and sexual slavery, along with evidence from another 200 interviews, were recorded by the commission, which stated that due to strong cultural reasons for underreporting, the total number of sexual violations was likely to be several times higher. The commission estimated that thousands, rather than hundreds, of women were subjected to serious sexual violations by members of the Indonesian security forces.

Exposing the "darkest memories"

The vast majority of women interviewed by the commission were young at the time they were violated. They were middle-aged at the time of giving their evidence to the commission. "Many said that they had harboured their darkest memories in silence during the long intervening years. The process of bringing this evidence to the Commission often involved a difficult emotional process for them." Despite the considerable cultural taboos, a number of women gave detailed accounts of their ordeals at public hearings, which were broadcast live by national radio and television services. Fourteen women told their stories at the commission's National Public Hearing on Women and Conflict, 28-29 April 2003.

The findings of the Chenga! report also draw the "inescapable conclusion", not surprisingly, that the hundreds of women who gave direct evidence represent only a portion of the total number of victims who did not give statements "because of social or personal pressures or an inability to talk about their experiences due to ongoing trauma connected to the violations."[36]

In-depth interviews and statements depicted an overwhelming picture of impunity for sexual abuse. The voices of the victims provided a clear picture of the widespread and systematic nature in which members of the Indonesian security forces openly engaged in rape, sexual torture, sexual slavery and other forms of sexual violence throughout the entire 24-year period of invasion and occupation. Sexual crimes were demonstrably encouraged and accepted (and practised) by military and police commanders. The victims' testimonies showed that there was a widely accepted practice for members of the security forces to rape and sexually torture women while on official duty in military installations and other official buildings.

The chronology of violations

According to the Chenga! Report, all but a few of the cases of rape documented by the commission were committed during the Indonesian occupation of Timor-Leste. Of these, 51 percent of rapes were committed during the invasion and the initial years of the occupation, and 23 percent occurred between 1985 and 1998. The remaining 26 percent of rapes were committed during the ballot-related violence in 1999, over a period of some few months.[37]

Data gathered by the commission show a sharp increase in rape cases in 1999, with peaks in April and September 1999. Of reported rapes from this year, 19 percent were committed by militia members. Data suggests that violence peaked again during the period following the announcement of the results of the plebiscite on 4 September 1999.

Rape took place along with forced displacement, house burning, killings, disappearances and other acts of violence. Some testimonies indicated that "rape centres" — places where women were forcibly detained and made accessible for repeated rape — existed in the midst of the violence during and after the Popular Consultation.

According to one woman's testimony, "On 10 September 1999, the militia and TNI [the Indonesian military] arrived at the house armed with weapons and threatened to kill me and all my family if I did not follow them to the militia headquarters. As we were all in a state of fear and panic, in the end I gave in. My father, mother and daughter resigned themselves to [my arrest]. [At] militia headquarters the militia handed

me over to three TNI soldiers who raped me for three days and three nights, from 10 to 12 September 1999".[38]

A similar testimony illustrates the specific naming (by code) of perpetrators, who were often known to the victims, which typifies the report: "On 7 September 1999, Irene saw two women, DF and EF, taken away forcibly by Laksaur militia known as PS186, PS187 and PS188. The three men beat DF severely until her mouth and nose were bleeding. Eventually DF fell to the ground and there she was raped while unconscious. As a result of the beating, the victim haemorrhaged for four months and then died."

For those forcibly detained or enslaved, "There was never a day without rape. At any time, any day, my friends and I were raped," said one witness/victim. Another woman also explained how the soldiers and militia did not spare pregnant and lactating mothers: "I was not the only one raped. There were also women still breastfeeding, women whose children were a couple of months old and others whose children were three or four years old. When the soldiers raped the women, they took them outside and separated them from the children. Even if the children were crying, the soldiers did not care. All they wanted was to satisfy their lust. They also raped pregnant women."[39]

> "I was not the only one raped. There were also women still breastfeeding, women whose children were a couple of months old and others whose children were three or four years old."

These findings have been selected from the report's section dealing with sexual violence and illustrate the scope and detail of truth and reconciliation reports. In terms of recognition and exposure of the extent of the crime committed, they are considered critical to the process of justice and reconciliation and represent a new approach to highlighting the needs of victims of such crimes as well as the need to hold individuals responsible for their crimes. However, this is the first stage of the process and arguably the easiest. It is in the follow-up of findings and the implementation of recommendations where truth commissions often fail to deliver results as political interests restrict action.

The Chenga! recommendations

According to the mandate of the CAVR process, the Chenga! report was obliged to conclude with recommendations "concerning reforms and other measures whether legal, political or administrative which could be

Armed combatants of international or civil wars — whether a young recruit in a poorly resourced new army of a developing nation (above), or a professional soldier in the army of the United States (right) — are deployed in conflicts of their government's choosing and are required to follow orders that may entail transgressions of international humanitarian law. In many conflicts in poor, developing nations, the combatants of the official army as well as the rebel or militia forces may be coerced recruits. They may be forced to commit atrocities or participate in rape and sexual violence. In the case of child soldiers, the recruitment and abduction from their communities is often sealed by forcing them to commit an atrocity against their village or family to negate their chances of return.

Images: Brent Stirton (Sierra Leone and Iraq)

taken to achieve the objectives of the Commission, to prevent the repetition of human rights violations and to respond to the needs of victims of human rights violations."[40]

The CAVR recommendations are numerous and extensive and address the international community; specific countries; the promotion of human rights; reconciliation, justice and truth; national reform; and reparations for victims of violence and abuse. In relation to women and girls who were victims of sexual abuse, the CAVR recommendations are specific and offer limited, though tangible, benefits.

CAVR attempted to guarantee women's involvement at national and district levels through the participation of women commissioners and staff in both healing workshops and the CAVR's Urgent Reparations Programme.[41] The percentage of women identified as beneficiaries of the reparations programme was relatively low at 23 percent, in part due to cultural barriers, limited access to information and the presumption that men represented families' experiences of the conflict,[42] according to the International Centre for Transitional Justice (ICTJ). However, a number of successes have been noted. A Working Group on Victim Support, consisting of four female members out of seven, designed the programme, which provided individual reparations for victims of killing, disappearance, detention, torture, rape and "other forms of sexual violence".[43] In addition, funds were also provided to local organisations to provide services for the victims.

CAVR recommended giving at least 50 percent of reparations to female beneficiaries and giving reparations to "the most vulnerable from those who continue to suffer the consequences of gross human rights violations"[44] from 1974-1999, which in practice led to the prioritisation of funding for many widows, women with disabilities, those affected by severe trauma, victims of sexual violence and single mothers, some of whom had borne children as a result of rape.[45] The broad definition of sexual violence also included victims of rape as both men and women, as well as sexual slavery, forced marriage and other acts.[46]

Other truth and reconciliation processes in the Republic of South Africa, Haiti and Burundi have also struggled to go beyond the process itself and either deliver the recommended reforms and/or reparation, or successfully prosecute the major perpetrators of human rights abuses and other crimes. In Timor-Leste, the mechanisms are being developed to implement the international and institutional reforms recommended by the CAVR, but the national parliament has yet to approve the process. The release of the Chenga! report in 2006 was surrounded with controversy as senior public figures, champions of the independence struggle and victims of abuse themselves, distanced themselves from the reports' recommendations as political interests and strategic considerations appeared more important.

Observers of truth and reconciliation processes as part of transitional justice are still divided as to the success or failure of these mechanisms to produce genuine change and deliver justice to people emerging from abusive regimes or periods of conflict. Currently, the issue of local reconciliation processes versus international legal mechanisms are found to be at loggerheads in northern Uganda, where local communities wanting peace, at the expense of immediate justice, find the Rome Statute and the International Criminal Court to be major obstacles. Post-conflict justice is historically and methodologically at a very early stage in its evolution, and its future appears fraught with major political hurdles. ■

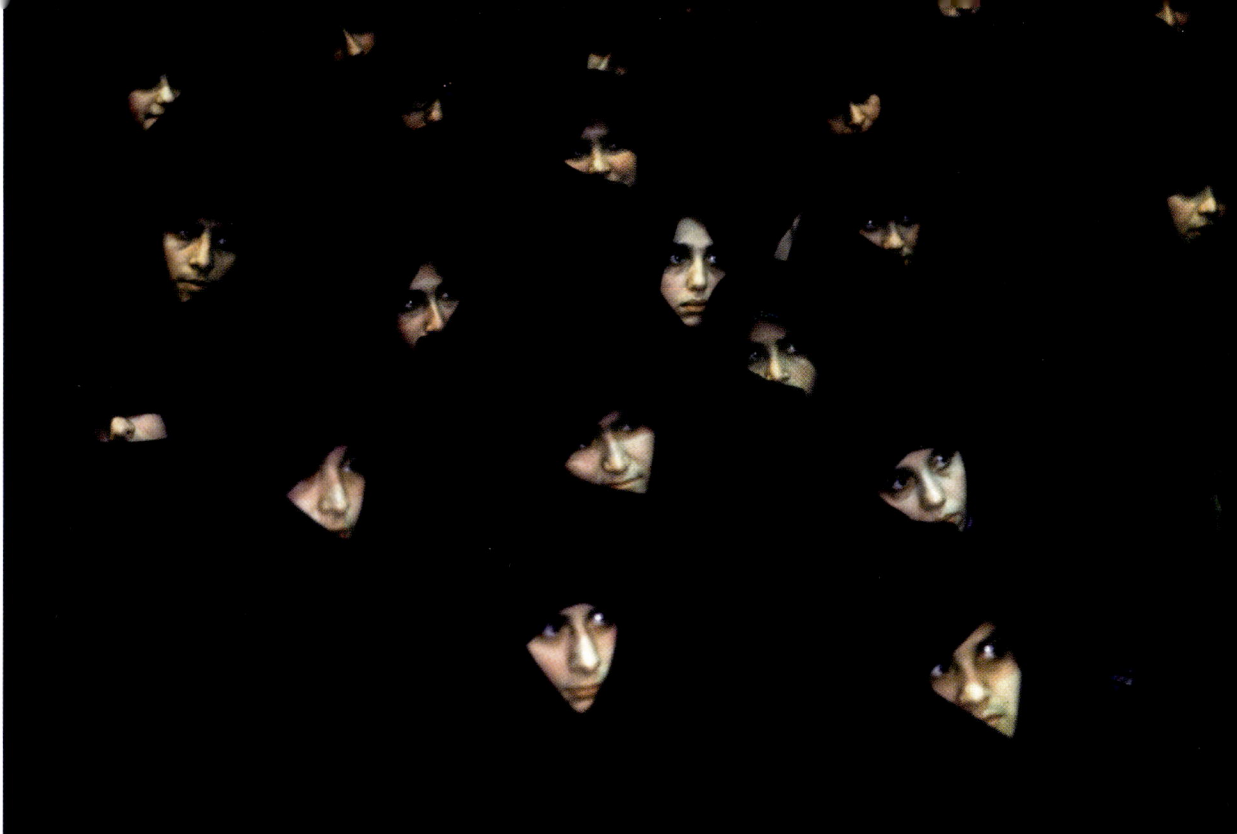

This photo was taken 20 years ago in the women's section of the notorious Evin political prison, in the northern suburbs of the Iranian capital. Extreme vulnerability for women and girls occurs in conflict, including in times of violent transition, such as the emergence of the Taliban in Afghanistan, the changing political climate in Haiti or, in this case, the rise of the Iranian Islamic Revolution in 1979. According to the photographer and many witnesses, prisoners who survived and guards who later revealed details, the young women in this image were among hundreds who were executed by the fundamentalist regime. All girls were raped by the guards the night before execution in order that the authorities should not be guilty of transgressing an alleged religious rule that virgins cannot be executed.

Image: Manoocher Deghati / IRIN

In Goma, Democratic Republic of Congo (DRC), a combatant mingles with young girls. In contexts of prolonged conflict, civilians and armed groups live in close proximity. In cultures where the proliferation of low-cost small arms makes weapons very accessible, the prevalence of rape and sexual violence is often high, as men use guns to obtain food, money and sex. In the case of eastern DRC, medical practitioners dealing with sexual violence claim that despite the end of hostilities the rate of violent rape of women, girls and even infants continues in a "smash-and-grab" culture brought about by chaos and guns.

Image: Sylvia Spring / IRIN

"Helena" is 25 years old and the victim of rape by a soldier in Sake, Democratic Republic of Congo. Her daughter "Fara", the child of the rape, is two-and-a-half years old.

"I was sent to buy salt one night and was grabbed by a group of soldiers hanging around by the market. They dragged me to a disused house nearby, where they regularly raped people they had taken from the market. There were 10 men, one of whom raped me. He pushed me to the floor and beat me, helped by the others. I told the man that I was a child and didn't want to do such things, but he just carried on. I felt so much pain in my stomach. I was taken by force to Kimbumba, 30 kilometres from Goma, where he kept me for a week until he was sent to war. I was left there, pregnant with his child. My parents had thought I'd disappeared so they welcomed me back into the home when I returned. But I have many problems: I rely on my mother for food, but sometimes we don't eat at all. I feel rejected by society because of what happened."

Image: Georgina Cranston

Gender-based violence against women and girls is commonplace around the world in peacetime and in war. Globally, at least one in every three women has been beaten, coerced into sex or abused in some other way. Conflict frequently exacerbates the violence many girls and women already face in their daily lives. In this photo, a woman flees the sporadic violence that surrounded the first-ever multiparty election in the Democratic Republic of Congo on 30 July 2006.

Image: Eddie Isango / IRIN

neglected challenges:
the humanitarian responsibility to protect[1]

Jan Egeland, then Emergency Relief Coordinator for the UN, visiting the Democratic Republic of Congo's eastern borderlands, where violence continues despite the official end to a 1996-2002 war, condemned the ongoing sexual violence against women and girls in the region. "Rape has become gangrene in Congolese society. [...] The armed men in government uniforms or [other] armed groups must know that rape is a crime against humanity that must be punished," he said after visiting a hospital where officials said more than 10,000 women had been treated for sexual violence since 1999. "The civilian population must be protected." (Sunday Standard report; 29 January 2007)

The humanitarian responsibility to protect against sexual violence in conflict

The World Summit of 2005 committed the United Nation's member nations to the shared responsibility of protecting populations from genocide, war crimes, ethnic cleansing and crimes against humanity. But unmitigated violence against women and girls in other new and ongoing conflicts and post-conflict settings around the world continues to emphasise the international community's failure to protect against sexual violence. Targeted violence of this scale requires much more effective and concerted action at global and local levels to speak out against sexual violence; provide security, safety and support to victims; and pursue legal recourse against perpetrators.

Gender-based violence, including sexual violence, is commonplace in the lives of girls and women around the world in peacetime and in war.

Globally, at least one in every three women has been beaten, coerced into sex, or abused in some other way.[2] Violence against girls and women is rooted in beliefs and attitudes about their subordinate status and their ongoing disempowerment.[3] Women and girls' inequality, low status and limited decision-making power in their homes and societies, the scarcity of women in leadership positions in every region of the world and poverty contribute to a climate in which women and girls can be violated with impunity.

Conflict frequently exacerbates the violence that many girls and women already face in their daily lives. Women and girls caught up in conflict, like other civilians, must battle disease, poor nutrition and a lack of shelter and healthcare. But during conflict, in flight and in refugee and displaced settings, they are also extremely vulnerable to gender-based

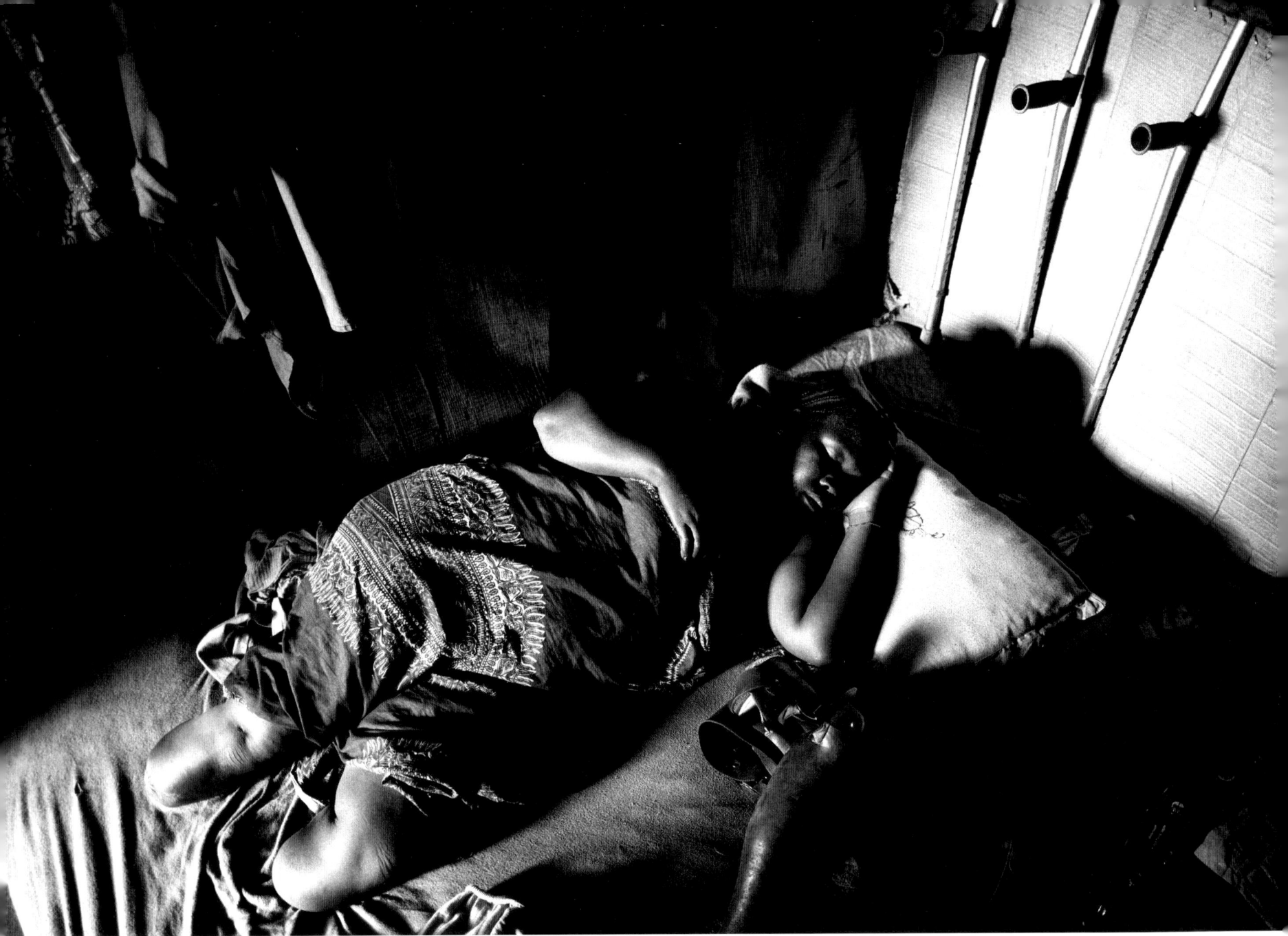

Rape and mutilation during the bloody conflicts in Sierra Leone and Liberia were commonplace. More than 100,000 men, women and children were deliberately mutilated, including this woman from Sierra Leone. In Liberia, reports of sexual attacks against girls and women are as high as 70 percent of all females. Truth and reconciliation commissions and special courts to bring to justice a handful of the faction leaders offer little reparation, restitution or solace to victims who struggle to survive with their memories, humiliations, scars and disabilities.

Image: Brent Stirton

violence. As war-related violence escalates, women and girls are often singled out and targeted for rape, sexual slavery, prostitution, domestic violence, trafficking and forced pregnancy. Survivors[4] of sexual violence can sustain serious physical injuries and psychological trauma as a result of the violence they have endured yet they usually have few means of seeking justice, medical care or psychosocial support.

This chapter examines the international community's current response to sexual violence in conflict-affected countries, identifying gaps as well as renewed efforts to scale up measures to meet the needs of victims/survivors in a timely and compassionate manner. Specific reference to the problem of sexual violence in Darfur, Sudan, highlighted in this article emphasises the urgent need for strengthened and coordinated action by humanitarian and other actors in a number of areas to prevent and respond to gender-based violence in all its forms. Much more needs to be done, for example, to address the medical and psychological impact of sexual violence on individual victims as well as on communities. The majority of victims continue to be unable to access appropriate care and support services or pursue legal recourse for the crimes committed against them. Most critical, however, is the need to address long-term gender inequality and ongoing discrimination against women and girls, which allows sexual violence to go unpunished and victims to suffer in silence and in shame.

Sexual violence in conflict

During conflict, girls and women are subjected to sexual assault with alarming frequency. In most conflict settings, sexual violence has been considered a "by product" of war: girls and women are sexually assaulted by soldiers, militia, police, security officials, local leaders, fellow refugees or displaced persons, members of the host community and even family members as impunity for sexual violence crimes continues.

The use of rape as a weapon of warfare and tool of "ethnic cleansing", including through forced pregnancy, has been documented in the recent wars in Bosnia and Herzegovina, Croatia, and Rwanda.[5] In Rwanda, it is estimated that at least 250,000 girls and women were raped during the 1994 genocide.[6] In Democratic Republic of Congo (DRC), rape is used by armed forces and groups to gain territorial control through displacement and establishing a stranglehold of fear over villages. Practitioners working as health service providers to survivors have

described sexual violence in the DRC as a form of "psychological destruction" designed to terrorise victims, their families and their villages.[7] Catharine MacKinnon argued that during the conflict in Bosnia and during World War II, rape was used as a tool of genocidal warfare.[8] Both rape and genocide, she said, create disassociation and compliance, with a concomitant desire to propitiate the potential captor/rapist and vitiate social bonds.

Globally, at least one in every three women has been beaten, coerced into sex, or abused in some other way. Violence against girls and women is rooted in beliefs and attitudes about their subordinate status and their ongoing disempowerment.

Incidents of rape fuel tensions amongst ethnic groups and contribute to a heightened climate of insecurity in displacement settings in Liberia, the Central African Republic and Burundi. Most survivors face serious difficulties in not only seeking the support they deserve, but also being accepted by their communities and families afterwards. Heightened levels of domestic violence are also increasingly being recognised as a feature of conflict and post-conflict settings. Domestic violence may be adopted as a form of "punishment" in the home for a lack of food provisions, limited resources or a general sense of frustration within families.

Rape has also been perpetrated by those whose mandate it is to protect. UN peacekeeping troops and humanitarian personnel have committed rape and other acts of sexual exploitation and abuse in a number of humanitarian and other operations. Crises' affect on livelihoods, coupled with a general lack of income opportunities in poverty-stricken environments, has forced many women and girls, especially adolescent girls, to turn to prostitution with wealthy and relatively more powerful aid workers and peacekeepers.

In 2005, the UN Secretary-General's special advisor, Prince Hussein of Jordan, conducted an investigation into the problem in the DRC and found that sexual exploitation and abuse by peacekeepers was "rampant" and had brought shame upon the name of the United Nations. The most frequent form of abuse and exploitation by members of the UN peacekeeping mission in the DRC (MONUC) was found to be prostitution (with both women and children), "occasional instances of rape" and "'rape disguised as prostitution,' where a girl was raped and then given money or food to give the appearance of a transaction." Victims giving birth to children as a result of rape frequently face ostracism by their families and communities as a result. Their children are at real risk of being denied access to education and basic health services and being marginalized from their communities in the long term.

The case of Darfur: a failure to protect or deliver services

Gender-based violence, including rape, has been publicised as a widespread and systematic feature of the conflict in Darfur, Sudan. The International Commission of Inquiry in 2005 concluded that rape and sexual violence had been used by government forces and government-backed Janjawid militia as a "deliberate strategy with the aim of

In attacks documented by Human Rights Watch, girls as young as seven and eight years old were raped, while some women were raped and then genitally mutilated.

terrorizing the population, ensuring control of the movement of the IDP [internally displaced peoples] population and perpetuating its displacement."[9] In attacks documented by Human Rights Watch, girls as young as seven and eight years old were raped, while some women were raped and then genitally mutilated.[10] Yet, despite the rhetorical prevalence of this issue, rape continues on a widespread and systematic scale with impunity in Darfur.[11] Many victims are children. Doctors from Médecins Sans Frontières in 2005 reported having treated almost 500 rape victims in a five-month period in one of their clinics in Darfur and were then expelled for releasing a public report to this effect. Assessments of the situation in displaced settings in the region indicate that the problem, first noted in 2003, continues virtually unabated and may even be getting worse.

According to a public statement by the International Rescue Committee in August 2006, "More than 200 women have been sexually assaulted in the last five weeks alone around Darfur's largest displaced camp, Kalma [...] This is a massive spike in figures. We are used to hearing of 2 to 4 incidents of sexual assault per month in Kalma camp." The women of Darfur are particularly vulnerable. They have no choice but to leave their camp confines in search of firewood – expeditions that force them to walk several miles into the bush. If men went instead, they would be killed. "We [...] have chosen to risk being raped rather than let the men risk being killed," one woman said summarizing how hopeless their plight has become."[12]

These figures are only indicative, however, as rape is grossly underreported in Darfur – as in many other contexts. The World Bank estimates that less than 10 percent of sexual-violence cases in non-refugee settings are reported.[13] Any available data will represent therefore only a small proportion of actual incidents of sexual violence.[14] Barriers to reporting and other response challenges in Darfur include:

i) Lack of services and monitoring and reporting mechanisms: Given the great sense of shame, humiliation and fear felt by victims of sexual violence, the majority of whom are women and girls,[15] in seeking care and support, as well as the risks of further harassment and intimidation, reporting is unlikely to improve and numbers of victims of gender-based violence likely to remain impossible to quantify. Many continue to be discouraged from seeking legal redress for the crimes committed against them, and there are complications concerning when and how to report, as well as necessary documentation for accessing medical care.[16] Service providers (local or international) are also frequently under harassment themselves. Collaboration between NGO and UN actors is often difficult in this challenging political and security environment. Without adequate services that allow and encourage appropriate monitoring systems, denial of the scope and scale of the problem by authorities and parties to the conflict persist.

ii) Impunity for perpetrators: Female victims of sexual crimes in Darfur are further victimised by often cumbersome, contradictory and discriminatory proceedings within the legal justice system. For example legal aid for victims is rarely available and only provided to victims during investigative procedures if they are under 18 years of age according to the Sudan Child Act of 2004. Until a recently, a victim had to first ensure signature of a medical examination by a certified doctor, although medical staff are desperately lacking. Victims must provide proof of age and are sometimes subjected to forced "medical exams" to determine their eligibility to a guardian, welfare officer or legal representative during police questioning. Such questioning is often re-victimising for survivors and can result in prolonged periods of detention. As in other countries practicing Sharia, or traditional Islamic law, if an unmarried woman or girl is pregnant and cannot prove that she was raped, she can be charged with the capital crime of adultery. To convict a man of the same offence, a confession or the testimony of four witnesses is required. For all these reasons, perpetrators are rarely held to account. At the time of writing, only one conviction for sexual violence had been prosecuted in Darfur since the crisis unfolded in 2003, despite reports of many thousands of rapes.

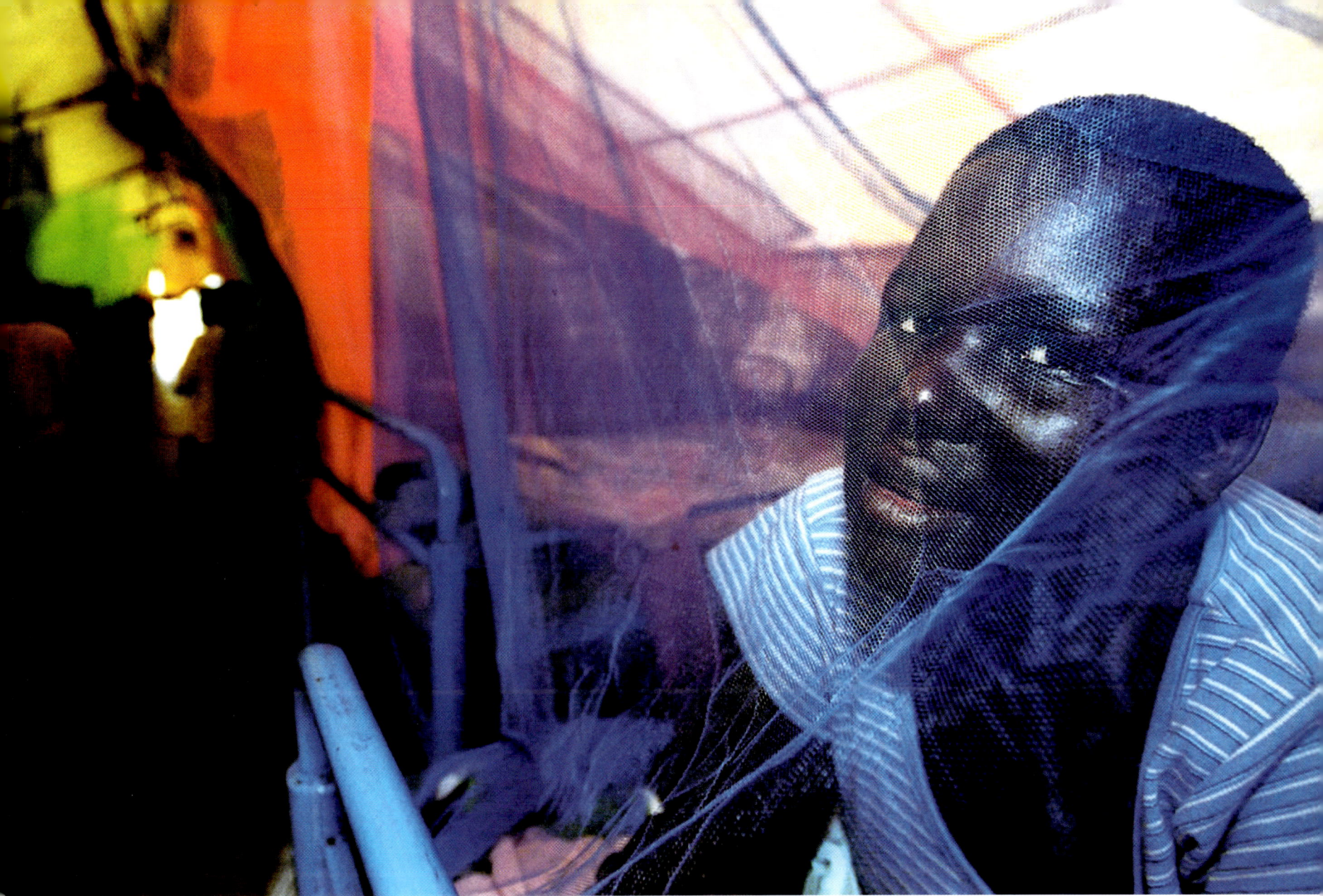

A recently freed former "bush wife" of the Lord's Resistance Army (LRA) in northern Uganda finds help at the Gusco Rehabilitation Centre. Recent reports suggest that as many as 66,000 children were abducted by the LRA during the last two decades. Boys were used as soldiers and porters, while girls were enslaved as domestic workers, raped and normally given to LRA commanders as "wives". Despite the work of centres like Gusco, the future of returned girls, many of whom have borne the children of their captors, is uncertain as they seek to re-enter a traditional society where men are unlikely to marry or care for girls with experiences such as these. What protection do they have for the future? What economic options and what justice, if any, can they expect?

Image: Sven Torfinn/OCHA

Commercial sex workers in Freetown, Sierra Leone. The youngest of these three girls is 10 years old. She works in the dock area and goes out to the foreign fishing ships. She has to have sex with the ferry captain to get to the ships, is often raped while out there and comes back with no money, and has to have sex with the ferry captain again to return to shore. Prostitution and rape have also led to a large number of abandoned and malnourished children. Having been sexually abused during the war, many girls and women have been separated from their communities and now face continued sexual exploitation and abuse during peace time.

Image: Brent Stirton

Despite overwhelming evidence of sexual violence in and around camp perimeters in Darfur, the international community has failed to act collectively and decisively to respond to the plight of women and girls at risk. More than $600 million in foreign aid, or about $89 per person,

Many girls and women lose their family and community after experiencing rape due to feelings of shame and discriminatory attitudes. Their only option may be further victimisation through sexual exploitation.

has been given to address the Darfur crisis, yet women and girls continue to be unsafe when they leave camp perimeters to collect firewood, as well as in their own homes, where they are subject to beatings and abuse. Anecdotal evidence from operational UN agencies and NGO partners in Darfur has pointed to an increase in domestic violence when food rations have decreased at various stages of the relief effort.

Principles of health, psychosocial and legal support

It is imperative that the international community, including governments and international aid agencies, recognises the impact of sexual violence and provides access to appropriate services for all victims and survivors. Victims of violence have a right to access healthcare and support services that respond to injuries, protect them from further harm and address long-term needs caused by the violations.

The UN Secretary General's In-depth Study on All Forms of Violence Against Women (2006) lays out specific guiding principles for provision of services to assist women and girls who have experienced violence as follows:

- Promote the well-being, physical safety and economic security of victims/survivors and enable women to overcome the multiple consequences of violence to rebuild their lives;
- Ensure that victims/survivors have access to appropriate services and that a wide range of support options are available that take into account the particular access needs of women facing multiple discrimination;
- Ensure that service providers are skilled, gender-sensitive, have ongoing training and conduct their work in accordance with clear guidelines, protocols and ethics codes and, where possible, provide female staff;
- Maintain the confidentiality and privacy of the victim/survivor;
- Cooperate and coordinate with all other services for victims/survivors of violence;
- Monitor and evaluate the services provided;

- Reject ideologies that excuse or justify men's violence or blame victims;
- Empower women to take control of their lives.[17]

These principles apply to all situations, but where the state cannot meet its obligations to provide these services to victims, it is the responsibility of the international humanitarian community to intervene. The UN, committed to upholding the fundamental freedoms, dignity and human rights of all, has a particular policy and advocacy, as well as programmatic, role to play in preventing and responding to gender-based violence. Key areas for programmatic response are health, psychosocial and legal support described below:

i) Health: Responding to the devastating healthcare consequences of sexual violence is a key intervention and arguably the most critical. The health consequences of rape are many: sexually transmitted infections and reproductive health problems, unwanted pregnancy, fistulae, maternal mortality and HIV/AIDS. Post-rape care should be available, including Post Exposure Prophylaxis (PEP) for HIV/AIDS where a victim is at risk of contracting the virus. Victim health services should, where appropriate, be integrated into national and local health services to include private interviewing rooms. Training on caring for survivors for medical, counseling, legal and police staff should be provided.

ii) Psychosocial: The stigma attached to sexual-violence survivors often means that survivors feel they do not have anyone to whom they can turn. Women's groups can play an important role in providing local support and care by offering a community network and providing information and support. Local associations can also provide information to girls and women seeking health treatment. Such centres should also specifically address the needs of girls (and boys) of all ages. To assist girls and women in addressing the myriad of problems that survivors so frequently face, women's groups require more concerted support from the international humanitarian community. Efforts also need to be expanded on a global scale to increase survivors' access to social, educational and economic opportunities. Many girls and women lose their family and community after experiencing rape due to feelings of shame and discriminatory attitudes. Their only option may be further victimisation through sexual exploitation. In the case of Darfur, women and girls' economic value is closely linked to virginity, and many victims are therefore made to marry their rapist or forced to provide family income in other ways. Aid workers in DRC have reported that the most important assistance rape survivors lack is economic: resources to survive and rebuild their lives. Economic support and skills training is well within the capacity of governments and of the international aid community and could be a far more integral and expanded part of assistance to rape survivors. Income-generating and microcredit schemes can serve to empower survivors and are vital elements of a holistic support programme.

iii) Legal: Provision of victim services is both a human right and a means to facilitate justice at the national or international levels, yet there remains an almost absolute dearth of services in conflict-affected areas. In many countries, like Haiti and Burundi, girls and women rarely come forward to report sexual violence in the absence of

Recent initiatives and the challenge ahead

Despite the enormous prevention and response gaps, some progress has been made to raise the profile of gender-based violence, including sexual violence, on the international agenda. The Rome Statute of the International Criminal Court specifies that "rape, sexual slavery, enforced prostitution, forced pregnancy, enforced sterilization" or any other form of sexual violence of comparable gravity constitute war crimes and crimes against humanity. The International Criminal Tribunals for the former Yugoslavia and Rwanda have recognised sexual violence, including rape, as acts of torture, a crime against humanity and an element of genocide in some circumstances. The Rwanda tribunal recognised that "sexual violence is not limited to physical invasion of the human body and may include acts which do not involve penetration or even physical contact". The Special Court for Sierra Leone included forced marriage in an indictment.

Women specific projects accounted for only 0.07 percent of the $1.7 billion, UN-sponsored 2002 reconstruction plan in Afghanistan, for example.

concrete services to support their healing. Where these services do exist, few possess staff trained in interviewing and supporting sexual violence survivors so as to ensure compliance with international guiding principles of respect, confidentiality and the pursuit of the best interests of the survivor. This can have grave consequences for their safety, security and wellbeing. Good practice does exist, however, as in the Thutezela Care Centres in South Africa, which provide high-quality health, psychosocial and legal support under one roof, resulting in increased conviction rates for sexual assault.

Reparations to victims of sexual violence is frequently recommended in commission reports, truth and justice inquiries and human rights reports. Reparations have been discussed and recommended in countries such as Guatemala, Rwanda, Liberia, Haiti, Timor-Leste and many others, but there have been few if any pay-outs to date. The reality is that while recommendations are widely applauded they are rarely followed through if they have neither political support nor financial, often international, backing. However, during 2006, members of parliament in Sarajevo reportedly agreed to consider new legislation to establish a reparations system for victims who were raped during the 1992-1995 Bosnian war. The measure, which would pay out a monthly disability pension of between 70 and 200 euros per victim, is the first of its kind to be considered in the region and is expected to compensate an estimated 5,000 women already registered as rape victims in Bosnia.

When the UN Security Council unanimously adopted Resolution 1325 on Women and Peace and Security in October 2000, it was the first time it had addressed the disproportionate and devastating impact armed conflict has on women and girls. The resolution also recognised the often under-valued contributions women make to conflict prevention, peacekeeping, conflict resolution and peace building, and the need to ensure that women are involved in all stages of the peace process. In many countries, women are becoming more involved in post-conflict reconstruction processes. Still, many reconstruction efforts do not involve women or specifically focus on women. Women-specific projects accounted for only 0.07 percent of the $1.7 billion, UN-sponsored 2002 reconstruction plan in Afghanistan, for example. Much more must be done to strengthen enforcement of Security Council resolution 1325 to make it matter for girls and women on the ground.

The Security Council should act decisively to respond to violence against girls and women by including protective measures in resolutions, peacekeeping mandates and other key decisions and discussions. Jan Egeland, former Emergency Relief Coordinator for the UN, addressed the Security Council in 2006 and appealed for stronger reporting, full compliance and legal recourse related to Security Council Resolution 1325 and appealed to government leaders to "live up to their responsibilities" and hold military, political and administrative leaders accountable for acts of rape committed on their watch.

In 2006, the General Assembly endorsed a new resolution on strengthening the coordination of emergency humanitarian assistance of

Due to the unending insecurity in northern Uganda, some 1.6 million people currently are living in more than 200 camps for internally displaced persons. Residents at the camps report that mass displacement has had a disastrous effect on their society. Signs of the social breakdown include high levels of promiscuity, substance abuse, unprotected sex and increased numbers of child mothers. As people stay longer and longer in the camps, what is left of their dignity is gradually eroded. Disrespected by the traumatised youth, forced to look on, powerless, as their society is turned inside out by violence and fear, some of the older adults become mentally ill, according to camp leaders.

Image: Sven Torfinn/OCHA

A woman waits for treatment at a centre for women who have been raped in Goma, Democratic Republic of Congo. Medical, psychosocial and economic support for the thousands of women violently raped in conflict and post-conflict settings is considered by many experts as "woefully inadequate". The medical repercussions of brutal rape are considerable, including the frequent risk of contracting sexually transmitted infections and HIV/AIDS. Support for these women and girls can transform their lives and give them hope after the injustice and outrage of rape has destroyed their health, peace and social lives so completely.

Images: Georgina Cranston

the UN, which includes important language on the problem of gender-based violence, the need for increased prosecutions and the strengthening of support services for survivors.[18] In parallel, the Inter-agency Standing Committee (IASC) has developed draft guidelines on gender-based violence interventions in humanitarian settings for pilot testing in key locations in 2005, including in Colombia, Sudan and Uganda.

A number of organisations, like the International Rescue Committee, are increasingly investing in gender-based violence programming, and advocacy and partnerships between the UN and NGOs is expanding to include the development of an information-management system for gender-based violence incidents, to assist in better understanding both the nature and scope of gender-based violence as well as the quality of comprehensive care for survivors. A Caring for Survivors training programme for health workers, which includes medical, psychosocial and legal components, is being developed alongside guidance on confidentiality and safety issues.

Children's organisations are also starting to prioritise rape in war as a children's rights issue. In 2004, Unicef updated its core commitments to children – the minimum obligations to which Unicef commits itself during the initial phases of an emergency – to include protection from and response to sexual violence for the first time. New policy and programmatic advancements in this area have increased, and innovative programmatic and advocacy efforts are underway. Unicef is also leading the implementation of Security Council Resolution 1612 on monitoring and reporting grave violations against children affected by conflict, including sexual violence. While women's NGOs and UN agencies have prioritised sexual violence for a long time, it is a fairly recent phenomenon that children's organisations have given it the same attention, especially in view of the fact that at least half of rape victims in non-conflict settings are estimated to be under the age of 18.

In December 2006, a high-level meeting for UN and NGO senior managers as well as member state representatives was held to address sexual exploitation and abuse by UN staff and related personnel, including peacekeepers. Among the many positive outcomes of the meeting were express commitments to broaden gender-based violence response initiatives as well to implement the Secretary-General's recently issued Strategy on Assistance to Victims of Sexual Exploitation and Abuse by UN Staff and Related Personnel. UN agencies are also rallying together to launch a joint initiative to bolster the UN's response to gender-based violence in crisis and recovery settings.

Still, it would be naïve to ignore the fact that the movement to strengthen accountability mechanisms, provide tools and guidance for practitioners and better respond to the needs of survivors is at the beginning of its struggle. As argued in this chapter, rape is a consistent feature of many conflicts and recovery periods, and victims of sexual violence still face shame, stigma, inadequate victim services and enormous barriers to justice. Gender-based violence interventions are still grossly underfunded and fail to be incorporated into the majority of emergency responses. In its Consolidated Appeal Process (CAP) for 2006, Liberia received US$637,755 to support gender based violence projects, which was only 14 percent of the total funding requested for projects of this nature. In 2006, Burundi received none of the US$1,654,109 requested to fund gender based violence projects. Even where advances have been made in emergency operations, little is being done to respond to the increased violence characteristic of post-conflict, displaced and refugee settings such as Liberia[19], Burundi, Sierra Leone, Angola and Timor-Leste. Sexual exploitation – except that committed by UN staff and peacekeepers – and domestic violence remain almost completely ignored on the international humanitarian agenda.

Conclusion

As evidenced in Darfur and other contexts, addressing gender-based violence is a challenge in both peacetime and war. Addressing this crisis requires a response that includes immediate support measures for victims; access to legal services; and global, national and local advocacy to tackle embedded belief systems and social structures that discriminate against women and girls and allow sexual violence to continue unabated. Together these components form a comprehensive approach to sexual violence, which humanitarian and development actors have yet to fully adopt. Governments, donors and humanitarian agencies urgently need to harness the necessary resources – human and financial – to eliminate gender-based violence in all its forms and ensure that women and children can live in safety and dignity. Activists, advocates, policymakers, practitioners and other decision-makers must join forces to end this scourge that has no place in the 21st century. When states persistently violate human rights and when the international community fails to respond, it is a collective responsibility we have all failed to meet. ∎

Those working to support survivors of rape and sexual violence argue that much more can and should be done to assist those women brave enough to come forward for help. In addition to medical and psychosocial assistance, there is also a need to offer literacy, job training and microcredit and other income-generation programmes that empower women. Bringing to justice and punishing the perpetrators are rarely these women's priorities, as they are more concerned with their own daily struggle to maintain their health, feed themselves and their families, preserve their peace of mind and gain acceptance by their communities.

Images: Georgina Cranston

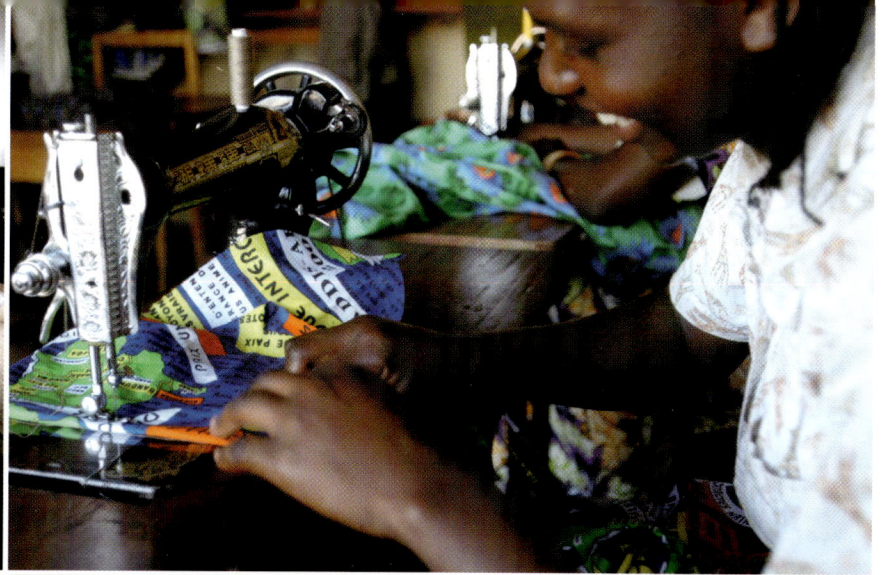

"Pewa" is 12 years old. Three years before this interview, she was raped in her home in Pinga, a village in northeastern Democratic Republic of Congo (DRC), by five Interhamwe militia. Interhamwe fighters, members of a Rwandan militia group responsible for the 1994 genocide, fled to neighbouring DRC following the genocide and have terrorised the local population.

"I have to live with the memory of being raped. The militia came one night at about 10 p.m., when we were sleeping. My mother and father were in one room and my two brothers, my sister and I were in the living room. They kicked down the door and came into the living room, so they saw us children first. There were five men. I was the first to be raped. They ordered me to take off all my clothes, including my underwear. I tried to refuse, but they told me they would shoot me. I was crying and refusing. I tried to run out, but they pushed me back with their hands, pointing their guns at me. I fell onto a mat on the floor. My brothers and sisters had run into my parents' room. The militia didn't touch them; they were very small. My parents tried to come out when this was happening to me but were forced back in. I was naked; the men had forced me to take my clothes off. Four of them were holding me down, one on each leg and one on each arm, while the other raped me. I was weeping so much. I couldn't stop thinking, Why hadn't we moved like other people? These men will give me diseases. I thought of HIV.

The men said nothing at all, the five of them raped me one after the other. I had terrible pain in my abdomen and vagina; I was bleeding. I just lay there — I couldn't move. When they had finished with me, they went into my parents' room. They beat my father and tied his hands behind his back and tied his legs. Then all five of the men raped my mother. My brothers and sisters and my father had to watch as they raped her. I was still in the other room on my own; all I could hear was all of them screaming. After they left, we sat up all night. We couldn't sleep and couldn't talk — we just sat in silence until morning. We left Pinga and came to Sake. I met a counsellor, and she sent me to Mweso Hospital [funded by Doctors On Call Services, a nongovernmental agency that provides medical treatment and counselling], where I was given medication. I had a disease but I don't know the name. I had abdominal, pelvic and vaginal pain and a thick, yellowish discharge. I'm better now, and my mother has also been treated and is OK. I am afraid to go out at night after what happened."

endnotes

Chapter 1 – sexual violence against women and girls in conflict

1 International Rescue Committee.(IRC) (2000); cited in J. Ward, 2002.

2 United Nations (UN) (2001); cited in J. Ward, 2002.

3 UN Special Rapporteur on Violence Against Women (2005); cited in J. Ward, "Gender-based Violence among Conflict-affected Populations: Humanitarian Program Responses," *Listening to the Silences: Women and War*, (Konnklikje Brill, Netherlands, 2005): 67.

4 S. Brownmiller (1975); cited in M. Hynes, J. Ward, K. Robertson and C. Crouse, "A Determination of the Prevalence of Gender-based Violence among Conflict-affected Populations in East Timor," *Disasters* Vol. 28 (3) (2004): 294-321.

7 S. Swiss and J. Geller, "Rape as a Crime of War: A medical perspective," *Journal of the American Medical Association* Vol. 279 (8) (1993): 625:629; World Health Organization (WHO) (1997); cited in Hynes and Lopes Cardozo, 2000; T. McGinn, "Reproductive Health of War-Affected Populations: What Do We Know?" *International Family Planning Perspectives* Vol. 26 (4) (December 2000).

6 J. Gardam and M. Jarvis (2001); cited in Amnesty International (AI), *Lives Blown Apart: Crimes Against Women in Times of Conflict* (London, 2004).

7 E. Rehn and E. Johnson Sirleaf, "Women, War, Peace," *Progress of the World's Women* 2002 Vol. 1 (2002): 4.

8 M. Vlachova and L. Biason, ed, *Women in an Insecure World: Violence Against Women, Facts, Figures, and Analysis*, Geneva Centre for the Democratic Control of Armed Forces (Geneva, 2005): 114.

9 Report of the Secretary-General on Women, Peace and Security, United Nations Security Council, S/2002/1154 (October 2002): 1.

10 T. McGinn (December 2000); AIDS Weekly Plus (1996); cited in Hynes and Lopes Cardozo, 2000.

11 Médecins Sans Frontières (MSF), "MSF shocked by arrest of head of mission in Sudan," MSF Press Release (Khartoum/Amsterdam, May 30, 2005).

12 M. Hynes, J. Ward, K. Robertson, C. Crouse, "A Determination of the Prevalence of Gender-based Violence among Conflict-affected Populations in East Timor," *Disasters* Vol. 28 (3) (2004): 294-321.

13 Avega (1999); cited in Ward (2002).

14 International Alert (IA) Press Release, "Panel on the Causes and Consequences of Sexual Violence against Women and Girls in South Kivu, Democratic Republic of Congo (New York, March 2004).

15 International Alert, Reseau des Femmes pour un Developpement Associatif and Reseau des Femmes pour la Defence des Droits et la Paix, *Women's Bodies as a Battleground: Sexual Violence Against Women and Girls during the war in the Democratic Republic of Congo* (2005).

16 International Alert et al, 2005, 34.

17 International Alert et al, 2005, 34.

18 Human Rights Watch (2000), cited in Ward (2002), 36.

19 PHR, 2002, 6.

20 International Alert, 2005, 11.

21 Integrated Regional Information Networks (IRIN), *Our bodies, their battleground: Gender-based Violence in Conflict Zones*, IRIN Web Special on violence against women and girls during armed conflict (September 2004).

22 Oxfam UK (2001); cited in Ward (2002).

23 R. Ojiambo Ochieng, "The Efforts of non-governmental organizations in assessing the violations of women's human rights in situations of armed conflict: the Isis-WICCE experience," Paper presented at the expert group meeting on Violence Against Women: Statistical Overview, Challenges and Gaps in Data Collection and Methodology and Approaches for Overcoming Them, UN Division for the Advancement of Women, (Geneva, April 11-14, 2005): 11.

24 AI, *Sudan, Darfur Rape as a weapon of war: Sexual violence and its consequences* (London, 2004): 15.

25 Rehn and Johnson Sirleaf, 2002, 2.

26 Shan Women's Action Network and Shan Human Rights Foundation, *License to Rape* (2002).

27 UN Spec. Rap. January 2001, p 27.

28 UN Spec. Rap. January 2001, p 28.

29 Watchlist on Children and Armed Conflict, *Colombia's War on Children* (February 2004).

30 Ward, 2002.

31 Rehn and Johnson Sirleaf, 2002, 17.

32 AI, *Sudan*, 2004, 12.

33 International Alert, 2005, 46.

34 IRIN, 2004, 22.

35 M. Hobson, *Forgotten Casualties of War: Girls in armed conflict*, Save the Children (London, 2005).

36 Watchlist, 2004.

37 AI, "Liberia: No Impunity for Rape, A Crime Against Humanity and a War Crime," (December 2004).

38 AI, *Casualties of War: women's bodies, women's lives: Stop crimes against women in armed conflict* (October 2004): 3.

39 Watchlist on Children and Armed Conflict, *Caught in the Middle: Mounting Violations Against children in Nepal's Armed Conflict* (New York, January 2005): 39.

40 Hobson, 2005, 10.

41 United Nations High Commissioner for Refugees (UNHCR), *Refugees By Numbers (2006 Edition)* (2007). Available from: www.unhcr.ch.

42 UN Security Council, *Report of the Secretary-General on women, peace and security* (October 2002): 2.

43 AI, *Forgotten Casualties of War*, 2005.

44 M. Vlachova and L. Biason, eds. *Women in an Insecure World: Violence Against Women: Facts, Figures and Analysis*, Geneva Center for the Democratic Control of Armed Forces (Geneva, 2005).

45 Vlachoya and Biason, 2005.

46 Watchlist, 2004; Ward, 2002.

47 Ward, 2002.

48 Watchlist, 2004.

49 Human Rights Documentation Unit and Burmese Women's Union (2000); cited in J. Ward (2002).

50 S. Olila, S. Igras and B. Monahan (October 1998); cited in T. McGinn, December 2000.

51 AI, *Liberia*, 2004, 4.

52 AI, *Forgotten Casualties of War*, 2004.

53 S. Nduna and L. Goodyear, *Pain Too Deep for Tears: Assessing the Prevalence of Sexual and Gender Violence Among Burundian Refugees in Tanzania*, IRC (New York, 1997).

54 AI, *Liberia*, 2004.

55 United Nations Children's Fund (Unicef), IRC, Christian Children's Fund, Legal Aid Project, "Protected Yet Insecure," unpublished document (November 2004): 20.

56 Reproductive Health Response in Conflict Consortium (RHRCC) et al, 2005.

57 UN Special Rapporteur on violence against women, its causes and consequences, *Integration of the Human Rights of Women and the Gender Perspective*, United Nations Economic and Social Council (January 2001): 29.

58 Spec. Rapp., 22.

59 Ward, 2002, 48.

60 A. Naik, "Protecting Children from the Protectors: Lessons from West Africa," *Forced Migration Review* Vol. 15 (October 2002): 17.

61 A. Naik, "UN investigation into sexual exploitation by aid workers," *Forced Migration Review* Vol. 16 (January 2003).

62 Human Rights Watch, *Iraq: Insecurity Driving Women Indoors* (2003).

63 AI, *Lives Blown Apart: Crimes Against women in times of conflict* (2004).

64 Hobson, 2005, 21.

65 AI, *Lives Blown Apart*, 2004.

66 IRIN, 2004.

67 AI, *Rwanda: "Marked for death," Rape Survivors Living with HIV/AIDS in Rwanda*, (April 2004): 9.

68 Ibid RHRC, *Gender-based Violence: Key Messages*. Available from: www.rhrc.org/rhr_basics/gbv.

69 AI, *Lives Blown Apart*, 2004.

70 AI, *Lives Blown Apart*, 2004.

71 UN, "Children and Armed Conflict: Report of the Secretary General pursuant to Security Council Resolution 1261" (July 2000); cited in Unicef, *The Impact of Conflict on Women and Girls in West and Central Africa and the Unicef Response* (February 2005): 21.

72 African Rights, "Broken Bodies, Torn Spirits: Living with Genocide, Rape and HIV/AIDS," Press Release (Kigali, April 2004): 4.

73 AI, *Lives Blown Apart*, 2004.

74 M. Hynes et al (2003) and M. Hynes (2004); cited in Reproductive Health Services for Refugees and Internally Displaced Persons, *Report of an Inter-agency Global Evaluation 2004* (November 2004): 39; RHRCC et al, 2005.

75 MSF, 2005, 6.

76 African Rights, 2004, 4.

77 African Rights, 2004, 5.

78 UNHCR, *Sexual and Gender Based Violence Against Refugees, Returnees and Internally Displaced Persons: Guidelines on Prevention and Response* (Geneva, May 2003).

79 Ward, 2002.

80 Rehn and Johnson-Sirleaf. 2002, xii.

81 UN Inter-Agency Standing Committee, *Action to Address Gender Based Violence in Emergencies: IASC Statement of Commitment* (January 2005).

82 K. Burnes, Personal Correspondence (11 July 2005); AI, *Lives Blown Apart*, 2004.

83 K. Burnes, Personal Correspondence (11 July 2005).

84 P. Donovan, "Rape and HIV/AIDS in Rwanda," *Supplement to The Lancet: Medicine and Conflict* (2002): 18.

Chapter 2 – perpetrators and motivation: understanding rape and sexual violence in war

1 D. Q. Thomas and E. R. Ralph, "Rape in War: Challenging the Tradition of Impunity," *SAIS Review* (Vol) (1994), 82-99. © The Johns Hopkins University Press.

2 G. J. McDougall, "Contemporary forms of Slavery; Systematic Rape, Sexual Slavery and Slavery-like Practices During Armed Conflict," final report submitted by the Special Rapporteur to the Commission on Human Rights (22 June 1998).

3 L.Heise, K.Moore, and N.Toubia, "Sexual Coercion and Reproductive Health: A focus on research," Population Council (1995).

4 Quoting from Chris McGreal, "A Pearl in Rwanda's Genocide Horror," The Guardian [UK], (5 December 2001).

5 "Sexual Violence within the Sierra Leone Conflict ," Human Rights Watch report (New York, 26 February 2001).

6 K. L. Cain, "Rape of Dinah: Human Rights, Civil War in Liberia, and Evil Triumphant," *Human Rights Quarterly* – Vol. 21, (2) (May 1999): 265-307.

7 D. Q. Thomas and R. E. Regan, "Rape in War: Challenging the Tradition of Impunity," *SAIS Review* (Vol) (1994), 82-99. © The Johns Hopkins University Press.

8 Observation by reviewer Themba Linden of Forum for Early Warning and Emergency Response (FEWER).

9 Certain sections of this article have been adapted from Chapter 14 of *Broken Bodies Broken Dreams – violence against women exposed*; IRIN/UNOCHA 2005, which deals with perpetrators of gender-based violence. Both articles were authored by Chris Horwood.

10 Findings taken from *The Roots of Behaviour in War; Understanding and Preventing IHL Violations*, ICRC (October 2005).

11 S. Whitworth, "Men, Militarism, and UN Peacekeeping: A Gendered Analysis" (2004).

12 Observation by reviewer Themba Linden of Forum for Early Warning and Emergency Response (FEWER).

13 A. N. Groth with H. J. Birnbaum, *Men Who Rape: The Psychology of the Offender*, (New York: Plenum Press, 1980).

14 W. McElroy, *The Reasonable Woman: A Guide to Intellectual Survival*, (1 April 1998), also at Lew Rockwell.com.

15 K. Stuhldreher, "State Rape: Representations of Rape in Vietnam," Political Science Department, University of Washington, Seattle. Vol. 5 (1-4) (March 1994).

16 These views are those of Studldreher (Ibid) and J. E. Lawson, " 'She's a pretty woman…

for a gook': The Misogyny of the Vietnam War," in P. K. Jason, ed., *Fourteen Landing Zones: Approaches to the Literature of the Vietnam War* (University of Iowa Press) 1991: 17.

[17] Thomas and Regan, 1994, (82-99).

[18] From review notes by Sarah Martin of Refugees International.

[19] M. Flood, "Deconstructing the culture of sexual assault," *Presentation to Practice and Prevention: Contemporary Issues in Adult Sexual Assault in New South Wales*, Sydney: University of Technology, 12-14 (February 2003).

[20] D. A. Counts, J. Brown and J. Campbell eds. *Sanctions and Sanctuary. Cultural Perspectives on the Beating of Wives*, Boulder, Colorado, (Westview Press) 1992. 268p as cited in IPPF Winter 2001 newsletter p.4.

[21] Flood, 2003.

[22] R. Thornhill and C. T. Palmer, "A Natural History of Rape: Biological Bases of Sexual Coercion," Cambridge MA (MIT Press) 2000.

[23] C. Paglia, *Sexual Personae: Art and Decadence from Nefertiti to Emily Dickinson*, (Random House) 1990.

[24] Refugees International http://www.refugeesinternational.org/content/article/detail/5944/?mission=5614.

[25] K. Carlson and D. Mazuran, "Young Mothers, Forced Marriage, and Children Born in Captivity with the LRA in Northern Uganda," *Disasters Journal*, publication forthcoming.

[26] "Sexual Violence within the Sierra Leone Conflict," Human Rights Watch report, (New York, 26 February 2001).

[27] Thornhill and Palmer, 2000.

[28] T. Susman, "Using rape as a weapon of war," Newsday Staff Correspondent (14 May 2006).

[29] Thomas and Regan, 1994 (82-99).

[30] D. Johnson, quotes from interviews in 2002 and quoted in "'Red Army troops raped even Russian women as they freed them from camps," Telegraph (on-line), (24 January 2002).

[31] Observation by reviewer Sarah Martin of Refugees International.

[32] S. Brownmiller, *Against Our Will: Men, Women and Rape* (New York: Simon and Schuster) 1975: 31.

[33] K. Stuhldreher, "State Rape: Representations of Rape in Vietnam," Political Science Department, University of Washington, Seattle. Vol 5 Number 1-4, (March 1994).

[34] Amnesty International, *Lives Blown Away*, (London) (December 2004).

[35] L. Hurst, "Rape a Deliberate War Strategy; Violence 'Must Stop' Amnesty Report Says," Toronto Star, (8 December 2004).

[36] Thomas and Regan, 1994 (82-99).

[37] B. Allen, *Rape Warfare: The Hidden Genocide in Bosnia-Herzegovina and Croatia* (1996).

[38] M. Danner, "America and the Bosnia Genocide," New York Review of Books, Vol. 44, Number 19 (4 December 1997).

[39] Thomas and Regan, 1994 (82-99).

[40] Thomas and Regan, 1994.

Chapter 3 – addressing impunity: sexual violence & international law

[ii] M. Graça, "The Impact of Armed Conflict on Children," United Nations report A/51/306, (September 1996) (para 91) http://www.un.org/children/conflict/english/themachelreport117.html.

[2] D. Q. Thomas and E. Ralph Regan, "Rape in War: Challenging the Tradition of Impunity," SAIS Review (Vol) (1994), 82-99. © The Johns Hopkins University Press. (para 30).

[3] G. J. McDougall, "Contemporary Forms of Slavery: Systematic rape, sexual slavery and slavery-like practices during armed conflict," Final report submitted by UN Special Rapporteur. UN Commission on Human Rights (22 June 1998).

[4] Hybrid courts, which emerged at the end of the 1990s, are considered to be the third generation of criminal bodies. The Nuremberg and Tokyo Tribunals were the first following World War II; the ad hoc ICTY and ICTR were the second. See Project on International Courts and Tribunals at <http://www.pict-pcti.org/courts/hybrid.html> for general introduction.

[5] See definition in Project on International Court andTribunals at http://www.pict-pcti.org/courts/hybrid.html.

[6] Ibid.

[7] Amnesty International, *The International Criminal Court, Fact Sheet 7, Ensuring Justice for Women*," AI Index 40/006/2005, (12 April 2005), available at http://web.amnesty.org/library/Index/ENGIOR400062005?open&of=ENG-373.

[8] R. Coomaraswamy, Report, UN Doc. E/CN.4/2003/75/Add.1, United Nations Special Rapporteur on Violence Against Women.

[9] See Max Planck Institute for Foreign and International Criminal Law, *National Prosecution of International Crimes*, available at http://www.iuscrim.mpg.de/forsch/straf/projekte/nationalstrafverfolgung2_e.html.

[10] See ICC, Frequently Asked Questions, available at < http://www.icc-cpi.int/about/ataglance/faq.html#faq4>.

[11] "A rule is customary if it reflects state practice and when there exists a conviction in the international community that such practice is required as a matter of law." See International Committee of the Red Cross, *Treaties and Customary International Humanitarian Law*, available at http://www.icrc.org/Web/Eng/siteeng0.nsf/htmlall/section_ihl_treaties_and_customary_law?OpenDocument.

[12] UN General Assembly Resolution 3074 (XXVIII), "Principles of international cooperation in the detention, arrest, extradition and punishment of persons guilty of war crimes and crimes against humanity".

[13] McDougall, 1998 (para. 91).

[14] McDougall, 1998 (para. 96).

[15] Thomas and Regan, 1994 (82-99).

[16] McDougall, 1998 (para. 92).

[17] McDougall, 1998 (para. 94).

[18] Human Rights Watch, *Kosovo Backgrounder: Sexual Violence as International Crime*, 10 May 1999, available at < http://www.hrw.org/backgrounder/eca/kos0510.htm>.

[19] Human Rights Watch, 1999. This may occur without double jeopardy occurring. Double jeopardy is a defence mechanism that forbids a defendant from being tried twice for the same crime.

[20] F. T. Pilch, "Sexual Violence During Armed Conflict: Institutional And Judicial Responses," GSC Quarterly (Summer 2002) available at http://www.ssrc.org/programs/gsc/gsc_quarterly/newsletter5/content/pilch.page>.

21 Pilch, 2002.

22 Thomas and Regan, 1994 (82-99) (para 14) Paraphrasing T. Meron, *Rape as a Crime under International Humanitarian Law*, JIL 87 No.3 424-428(1993).

23 Louise Arbour, chief prosecutor for the ICTR, CC/PIU/342-E, The Hague, 4 September 1998, available at http://www.un.org/icty/pressreal/p342-e.htm.

24 Arbour, 1998.

25 As defined in the 1948 Convention on the Prevention and Punishment of the Crime of Genocide.

26 *Akayesu*, ICTR trial chamber, 21 May 1999, para 95.

27 International Committee of the Red Cross (ICRC), *Treaties and Customary International Humanitarian Law*, available at http://www.icrc.org/Web/Eng/siteeng0.nsf/htmlall/section_ihl_treaties_and_customary_law?OpenDocument.

28 ICRC, *Treaties and Customary Law*, available at http://www.icrc.org/Web/Eng/siteeng0.nsf/html/genevaconventions.

29 F. Bouchet-Saulnier, Introduction to International Humanitarian Law, in Crimes of War Project, *Crimes of War: What the Public Should Know*, available at http://www.crimesofwar.org/thebook/intro-ihl.html.

30 Bouchet-Saulnier.

31 Bouchet-Saulnier.

32 Bouchet-Saulnier.

33 C. Moeller, *The Significance of the Ad Hoc Tribunals for the Establishment of a Permanent International Criminal Court: Prosecution of Sexual Violence in War and Armed Conflict*, International Society for Human Rights, available at http://www.ishr.org/activities/campaigns/icc/iccmoeller.htm.

34 (Prot 1, Art 75(2)(b), Prot 1 Art 76(1), and Prot 2, Art 4(2)(2).

35 H. Durham, "Women, Armed Conflict and International Law," International Review of the Red Cross, September 2002, Vol. 84, no 847, available at http://www.icrc.org/Web/Eng/siteeng0.nsf/iwpList139/B08F4F79CF15825741256C680035DBD0.

36 Durham, 2002.

37 Durham, 2002.

38 J. Gardam and M. Jarvis, *Women, Armed Conflict and International Law* (The Hague: Kluwer International, 2001) p 93.

39 *Delalic/Mucic/Delic/Landzo*, ICTY trial chamber, 16 November 1998.

40 Human Rights Watch, *Kosovo Backgrounder: Sexual Violence as International Crime*, 10 May 1999, available at < http://www.hrw.org/backgrounder/eca/kos0510.htm>.

41 Human Rights Watch, 1999.

42 *Furunzija*, ICTY trial chamber, 10 December 1998.

43 *Akayesu*, ICTR trial chamber, 2 September 1998, paras 596-598, 686-688.

44 A crime is composed of two elements, the *actus reus* (the act) and the *means rea* (the state of mind).

45 *Kunarac, Kovac, Vokovic*, ICTY trial chamber, 22 February 2001, para 460.

46 *Semanza*, ICTR trial chamber, 15 May 2003, para 344-345.

47 See *Celibici* and *Furundzija* trials at the ICTY.

48 R. J. LaShawn, *In War as In Peace: Sexual Violence and Women's Status*, 2004 World Report, Human Rights Watch, available at http://hrw.org/wr2k4/15.htm.

49 See War Crimes Studies Center, University of California Berkeley, Interim Report on the Special Court for Sierra Leone, April 2005, p 11-12.

50 *Akayesu*, ICTR trial chamber, 2 September 1998, para 597, 687.

51 *Semanza*, ICTR trial chamber, 15 May 2003, para 342-343.

52 Italics inserted, *Kvocka et al.*, ICTY trial chamber, 2 November 2001, para 186.

53 *Kupreskic et al.*, ICTY trial chamber, 14 January 2000, para. 624.

54 *Akayesu*, ICTY trial chamber, 2 September 1998, para 697.

55 *Prosecutor v. Mucic et al.*, ICTY trial chamber, 16 November 1998, para. 494-496.

56 *Kunarac, Kovac and Vokovic*, ICTY appeals chamber, 12 June 2002, para 142, 149-151.

57 Impregnation with the intent of forcing someone to give birth to a child.

58 Amnesty International, the International Criminal Court, Fact Sheet 7, Ensuring Justice for Women, 12 April 2005, AI Index IOR 40/006/2005 for the following analysis, available at http://web.amnesty.org/library/Index/ENGIOR400062005?open&of=ENG-373.

59 Amnesty International, 2005.

60 Amnesty International, 2005.

61 Amnesty International, 2005.

62 CEDAW committee, General Recommendation 19, para 6, available at http://www.un.org/womenwatch/daw/cedaw/recommendations/recomm.htm.

63 Beijing Declaration and Platform for Action, Fourth World Conference on Women, 15 September 1995, UN doc. A/CONF.177/20 (1995) and A/CONF.177/20/Add.1, available at http://www1.umn.edu/humanrts/instree/e5dplw.htm.

64 International Symposium on Sexual Violence in Conflict and Beyond, Brussels, 21-23 June 2006, para 6, available at < http://www.reliefweb.int/rw/lib.nsf/db900SID/EVOD-6RTHBF?OpenDocument>.

65 Adopted 31October 2000, available at http://www.un.org/events/res_1325e.pdf.

66 Article 2.

67 Article 11.

68 Thomas and Regan, 1994, 82-99 (para 17).

69 McDougall, 1998.

70 LaShawn, 2004.

71 LaShawn, 2004.

72 LaShawn, 2004.

Chapter 4 – sexual abuse and exploitation by peace-keepers and aid workers

1 John Bolton US representative to the UN in Feb 2006 referring to the problem of sexual abuse by peacekeepers.

2 Jane Holl Lute (assistant secretary-general for peacekeeping operations) as quoted in the BBC's *UN troops face child abuse claims*. 30 November 2006 www.bbc.co.uk.

3 "Human Rights Monitors Study Impact of Sexual Violence During Liberia's Civil War," UNPD press release (March 2004) as cited in "Must boys be boys? – Ending sexual exploitation and abuse in peacekeeping missions," a report by Refugees International (2005) page 3.

4 Review note added by Sarah Martin from Refugees International.

5 Refugees International, "Must boys be boys? – Ending sexual exploitation and abuse in peacekeeping missions," (2005) page 5.

[6] From communication with Sarah Martin of RI reflecting their meetings with representatives of member states.

[7] A.R. Kolbe and R.A. Hutson, "Human rights abuse and other criminal violations in Port-au-Prince, Haiti: a random survey of households" (August 2006).

[8] As quoted in the BBC report, "UN troops face child abuse claims" (30 November 2006), www.bbc.co.uk.

[9] "UN Peacekeepers in Haiti," The Lancet online (31 August 2006).

[10] D. Loyn, BBC Developing World correspondent, "Aid scandal hits Liberia's weakest," BBC News Online (7 May 2006).

[11] Nolan quoted in "Aid Workers Accused of Child Sex Abuse," Associated Press (27 February 2002).

[12] As quoted in "Aid-For-Sex Children Speak Out," BBC news (27 February 2003).

[13] As quoted in "Aid-For-Sex Children Speak Out," BBC news (27 February 2003).

[14] Quoted in "U.N. Slammed for Refugee Sex Scandal," NewsMax.com Wires (8 March 2002).

[15] Quoted in "Liberia sex-for-aid 'widespread,' " BBC News online (8 May 2006).

Chapter 5 – seeking post-conflict justice

[iv] E. Rehn and E. Johnson-Sirleaf, "Women, War and Peace: The Independent Experts' Assessment on the Impact of Armed Conflict on Women and Women's Role in Peace-building" (October 2002), p 91, available at http://www.reliefweb.int/rw/lib.nsf/db900SID/LGEL-5FMCM2/$FILE/unicef-WomenWarPeace.pdf?OpenElement>.

[2] See generally R. J. LaShawn, In War as in Peace: Sexual Violence and Women's Status, Human Rights Watch, World Report 2004, available at http://hrw.org/wr2k4/15.htm.

[3] Rehn and Johnson-Sirleaf, 2002 (p. 89).

[4] Rehn and Johnson-Sirleaf, 2002 (p. 89).

[5] Brussels Call to Action to Address Sexual Violence in Conflict and Beyond, 21-23 June 2006, available at http://www.unfpa.org/emergencies/symposium06/.

[6] B. Nowrojee, We Can Do Better Investigating and Prosecuting International Crimes of Sexual Violence, Paper presented at the Colloquium of Prosecutors of International Criminal Tribunals in Arusha, Tanzania, 25-27 November 2004, available at http://www.womensrightscoalition.org/publications/papers/doBetter_en.php.

[7] Rehn and Johnson-Sirleaf, 2002 (p. 97).

[8] HRW, LaShawn, 2004.

[9] In 2001, Physicians for Human Rights conducted a population-based assessment of the prevalence and impact of sexual violence and other human rights abuses among internally displaced persons in Sierra Leone. When their findings are extrapolated, the indications are that as many as 215,000 to 257,000 women and girls in Sierra Leone may have been affected by sexual violence. Some researchers claim the true figure is much higher.

[10] Information for case study provided in HRW report, R. J. LaShawn, In War as in Peace: Sexual Violence and Women's Status (2004). See also Amnesty International, Sierra Leone, Women Face Human Rights Abuses in the Informal Legal Sectory, AI Index: AFR 51/002/2006, (17 May 2006).

[11] Rehn and Johnson-Sirleaf, 2002 (p. 97).

[12] Rehn and Johnson-Sirleaf, 2002 (p. 97).

[13] Rehn and Johnson-Sirleaf, 2002 (pp. 97-98).

[14] Nowrojee, 2004.

[15] Nowrojee, 2004.

[16] Nowrojee, 2004.

[17] Rehn and Johnson-Sirleaf, 2002 (p. 95).

[18] The following points are abbreviated versions of those made in We Can Do Better Investigating and Prosecuting International Crimes of Sexual Violence, paper presented at the Colloquium of Prosecutors of International Criminal Tribunals in Arusha, Tanzania, 25-27 November 2004.

[19] Ibid.

[20] Ibid.

[21] B. Nowrojee, "Making the Invisible War Crime Visible: Post-Conflict Justice for Sierra Leone's Rape Victims," Harvard Human Rights Journal, (Vol. 18) (Spring 2005), available at http://www.law.harvard.edu/students/orgs/hrj/iss18/nowrojee.shtml.

[22] Paraphrased from the Introduction to "Truth Commissions and NGOs: The Essential Relationship, The "Frati Guidelines" for NGOs Engaging With Truth Commissions," the International Center for Transitional Justice (April 2004).

[23] United Nations Office of the High Commissioner for Human Rights (OHCHR), Rule-of-Law Tools for Post-Conflict States, Truth Commissions (2006) (p. 1), available at http://www.ohchr.org/english/about/publications/docs/ruleoflaw-TruthCommissions_en.pdf.

[24] OHCHR, 2006 (p. 2).

[25] Part III(6)(1).

[26] Rehn and Johnson-Sirleaf, 2002 (p.99).

[27] OHCHR, 2006 (p. 22).

[28] OHCHR, 2006 (p. 11).

[29] OHCHR, 2006 (p. 20).

[30] OHCHR, 2006 (p 20).

[31] OHCHR, Report of the International Commission of Inquiry on East Timor to the Secretary-General. Security Council report A/54/726, S/2000/59 (31 January 2000), http://www.unhchr.ch/huridocda/huridoca.nsf/(Symbol)/A.54.726,+S.2000.59.En.

[32] OHCHR, 2000 (paragraph 31-36).

[33] OHCHR, 2000 (paragraph 36).

[34] Chenga! (Enough!), Final report of the Commission for Reception, Truth and Reconciliation in East Timor (CAVR), p. 108.

[35] CAVR, p. 108.

[36] CAVR, chapter 7.7.

[37] CAVR, chapter 7.7.

[38] CAVR, chapter 7.7.

[39] All quotes from CAVR, chapter 7.7.

[40] Regulation 2001/10, section 21.2 of its founding resolution.

[41] International Centre for Transitional Justice (ICTJ), G. Wandita, K. Campbell-Nelson, M. Leong Pereira, Gender and Reparations in Timor-Leste, (p. 2), available at http://www.idrc.ca/uploads/user-S/11501298791TimorLesteExecSum.pdf.

[42] ICTJ (p. 4). Approximately US$160,000, or 3 percent of CAVR's total budget, was used for the programme.

[43] ICTJ (pp. 2-4).

44 CAVR, Final Report, Part 11, Recommendations, available at
< http://www.etan.org/news/2006/cavr.htm>.

45 ICTJ (p. 3).

46 ICTJ (p. 6).

Chapter 6 – neglected challenges:
the humanitarian responsibility to protect

1 Pamela Shifman and Lauren Rumble are currently working for UNICEF in New York in the
Child Protection and Emergency Operations sections respectively. This article reflects
the personal views of the authors and not necessarily of the organization.

2 UNFPA, 2000

3 While boys and sometimes men can be victims of gender - based violence, including sexual
violence, the majority of victims are girls and women because of their subordinate status.
Thus, girls and women are the focus of this chapter.

4 The terms victims/ survivors are used interchangeably in this chapter.

5 Graca Machel, *Impact of Armed Conflict on Children.*, 2001, p. 55.

6 E. Rehn and E. Johnson-Sirleaf, "Women, War and Peace: The Independent Experts
Assessment," UNIFEM (2002).

7 Interview with Dr. Denis Mukwege, director of the Panzi General Referral Hospital in
Bukavu, Democratic Republic of Congo, 1 December 2006, by Eve Ensler at the New
York University School of Law, New York.

8 C. Mackinnon, "Are Women Human? And Other International Dialogues," *Harvard Pounds*
(2006).

9 Report on the International Commission of Inquiry on Darfur to the United Nations
Secretary-General (25 January 2005) (p. 94), at
http://www.un.org/News/dh/sudan/com_inq_darfur.pdf.

10 Human Rights Watch, "Sexual Violence and Its Consequences Among Displaced Persons
in Darfur and Chad," briefing paper (12 April 2005).

11 See, for example, "Inter-agency Real-time Evaluation of the Humanitarian Response to the
Darfur Crisis: Observations and Recommendations," (p. 3) (DRAFT) (2 July 2005). See
also: Weekly Programmatic Brief for the Darfur Emergency - Week 28 (19 July 2005).

12 International Rescue Committee, M. Hartley, *Darfur's Downward Spiral* (23 August 2006).

13 "Reproductive Health in Refugee Situations: An Interagency Field Manual," 1999.

14 *(Draft)* Inter-Agency Standing Committee Guidelines (IASC) for Gender-Based Violence
(GBV) Interventions in Humanitarian Settings Focusing on Prevention of and Response
to Sexual Violence in Emergencies.

15 UNFPA & Unicef, Situational Analysis: The Effects of Conflict on the Health and Wellbeing of Women and Children in Darfur (2005).

16 See, for example, the Secretary-General's Monthly Report on Darfur issued 10 May 2005
(S/2005/305).

17 The Secretary-General's In-depth Study on all Forms of Violence Against Women was
launched in the General Assembly on 9 October 2006.

18 Draft United Nations policy statement and draft United Nations comprehensive Strategy
on Assistance to Victims of Sexual Exploitation and Abuse by UN Staff and Related
Personnel (A/60/877) (5 June 2006) General Assembly 60th Session, Agenda Item 2.
Available at: http://www.peacewomen.org/resources/Peacekeeping/SEA/victim_assis-
tance.pdf#search=%22%22A%2F60%2F877%22%22.

19 Save the Children-UK, "From Camp to Community: Liberia Study on Exploitation of
Children" (2006).

the shame of war

sexual violence against women and girls in conflict

HUSH

Whatever you do
Don't talk about it
Whatever you do child
Don't say a word
Your voice will echo through the walls and hills and will
Embarrass the community will
Shame the family
Do not tell them where that child came from

Though you have to stare into its eyes day and night
Suckling upon your bruised and empty breasts
Do not utter a word
Of its origin
Stay silent in your misery
Encompassed in your pain
Let your womb remain unheard
Verbs
Have no place here
Nouns
Have no face her
Adjectives and description
Will only cause questions and shame
So put this mask on child and remain still
Don't you dare show pain
Smile
And whatever you do
Don't talk about it
Whatever you do child don't make a sound

Even if the silence kills you inside
Even if the silence manifests in between your thighs into a disease
Baby don't you compromise your pride for your insides to feel
Free

You see,
This is what they told me
This
Is all I heard
Shame like concrete skyscrapers under constant construction in my soul
My laughter is of a clown
Frightening and insincere
I play with rubber erasers in attempts to erase all that took place
And most of all
To erase what they say

Because my voice contains power
My experience contains the experience of others
The birth of my words is the death of my shame
So I shall speak
Until my tongue goes numb
And my lips forget word
I shall speak
Until I create a hurricane and blow down concrete skyscraper
I shall speak
Through
Monologue
Through
Scripture
Through
Song
Through
Noise
Through
Bad blood
Through
My anger
Through
My pain
Through
My shame and yours
Through my soul
I shall speak
So I shall free
I shall speak
Through
Poetry

by Imani Woomera